Blast out of the Past!

RetroAge®

4 Steps to a Younger YOU!

HATTIE

with

Sallie Batson

RetroAge®

4 Steps to a Younger YOU!

RetroAge®

"I refuse to accept society's negative image of aging. That's the one you and I grew up with. If you give in and allow nature to take its usual course, you'll probably age as badly as you always feared you would. On the other hand, if you embrace aging as an exciting challenge, you can be the architect of your future… the victor over Time… not its victim."

Get ready for the adventure of a lifetime!
Yes, it's truly possible to reverse aging… starting NOW!

II

To book Hattie for events/appearances, private coaching and for information on services, cruises, rejuvenation vacations and products:

www.hattieretroage.com
212. 388. 8509

IV

DEDICATED TO

My grandchildren:

Nathaniel, Aden and Kika

Three great reasons for staying young!

VI

GRATEFUL TO

My lifeguards…in no particular order:

Those who know me well are aware of my passion for swimming. Below is an abbreviated list of some of the individuals who have kept me afloat. I thank them:

Josh Wiener, Rama Dunayevich, Sallie Batson, Zoila Suarez, Werner Erhard, Colleen Primrose, Alan Gumbs, Daniel Hall, Joel Benjamin, Fabiana Liburd, Girish Chandran, Eve Robinson, Nikita, Bernard Dunayevich, Pat Caparaso, Dr. Clifton, Dr. Kildahl, Dr. Vianna Muller, Dr. Crane, Dr. Berkowitz, Dr. Dana Cohen, Dr. Schwartzstein, Dr. Bissoon (By now you may be thinking, "this holistic fanatic sure has a lot of doctors." Well, you're right. But, in all fairness, some are dentists, physiotherapists, one ethno botanist…and shrinks!) Hattie Arnone, Martha Andrews, Rabbi Shmuley and Debbie Boteach, Francis Briggs, Anne Saxon-Hersh, Una Gumbs, Carrie Coakley, The Golem, Berni Cusack, Michele Kaufman, Elane Norych Geller, Dale Burg, Eric Pepin, Anne Fisher, Rebecca Levine, Ralph Lewin, Elena Rojas, Ben Marinucci, David Roman Daniels, Robert dePasquale, Joshua Plant, Carolina Fernandez, Bob Worth, Sally Keech, Justin Rand, Kimberly Armstrong, Cecily MacArthur, Jetty-Jane Connor, Rose Mollica, Tuvia Rothem, John Traynor, Donna Moore, Dan Whitten, Carnegie Hall ushers, staff of La Premiere.

…and my real life lifeguards at the Parker-Meridien Hotel pool - my New York City sanctuary for over 25 years: Anne, Carlos, Yolanda.

For my NY sanctuaries: MoMA, Parker-Meridien Hotel's Club Gravity, Central Park, Carnegie Hall, SOB's, Lincoln Center, Westerly Health Foods, Landmark Education, Cognac, Fiorellos, Candle Café, Molyvos and Mangia Restaurants, Silverlining Interiors, Daffy's, Central Park Physical Therapists. And for my blessed Caribbean island paradises: Rendezvous Bay, Anguilla

VIII

Table Of Contents

X

FOREWARD
Paving the Road to Youth

I had always viewed aging as a living death, but decline and decay were not what I envisioned as the perfect way to spend the second half of my life. Fortunately, rather than paralyzing me, my fears of aging propelled me into a lifelong search to avoid what I deemed inevitable. I have never been so glad to be proven wrong.

There comes a point in all of our lives that we become preoccupied with aging. A wrinkle here, a sag there, and pretty soon, we're off at the races. It happened to me when I got divorced at 48. Suddenly the face in the mirror wasn't the one I wanted to see. I felt old and ugly.

"This is horrible" I groaned, "It's all over for me." My mind went wild with worry. I saw myself morphing into a decrepit old woman. "What's going to happen to me? Are wrinkles and sagging skin gonna take over? "Is my sex life doomed?" I found myself obsessing about a future of lost health, beauty and sexuality. Fortunately, rather than discouraging me, it set me on a path to discover the fabled "Fountain of Youth."

For starters, I began reading everything I could find about aging gracefully. But aging gracefully wasn't what I had in mind. I didn't want to *accommodate* aging, I wanted to *reverse* it. Then, after trying countless techniques that didn't work, I knew I had to create my own answers. No way was aging going to turn me into a decrepit, sexless, old hag.

As a dancer, teacher and therapist, I'd always had a keen sense of my body. For decades I exercised, dry-brushed my skin and ate natural, Organic foods. I was careful about avoiding chemicals and toxins. The results had always paid off, but when I reached 50, I had to up the ante. It was time to swing into action and intensify the fitness and eating program that had worked so well for so long.

But working harder wasn't the answer either. The aging process was taking over...fast. My muscles were getting weaker, my skin was developing wrinkles, dryness and brown spots, and worst of all, my digestion got sluggish... UGH! I panicked.

One of my greatest blessings is that when faced with tough challenges I never let fear sabotage my resolve. In fact, it makes me even more resolute. Of course, like everyone else, I often feel frightened, especially when attempting something new. But time and time again, rather than holding me back, it provides me with the motivation to move ahead. My search was just beginning and I wasn't going to let fear stop me from finding the answers I was seeking.

I knew that if I were going to reverse the "natural" course of aging, I'd have to invent unconventional, radical techniques to get the job done. TV and magazines are filled with all sorts of "miracle" crèmes and lotions. Doctors are assuring us that Botox, surgery and shots will make us forever young. Instinctively, I knew this was all hype. True youth doesn't come from these distorted methods... it comes from within. What more proof do we need than seeing movie stars and models with expressionless, line-free surgically altered faces? That route was not for me.

Many of my techniques were way off the charts, as when I exfoliated dead skin with fine sandpaper, whacked my chest with a boxer's medicine ball or pounded my thighs with a rubber mallet. Yet, while seemingly weird, they were all safe, and achieved fantastic results. The more I practiced my far-out discoveries, the more convinced I became that they were going to powerfully reverse and retard the aging process – for me and for my clients and friends. The results didn't show right away, but after about two years the verdict was in. I not only *felt* much younger, I *looked* remarkably younger as well. And...I had no more cellulite!

Today, with over 20 years of RetroAge behind me, my quest has surpassed even my wildest dreams. Need proof? In December of 2008 and January of 2009, I was featured alongside Claudia Schiffer in a Dolce & Gabbana ad that appeared in VOGUE, Vanity Fair, Harper's Bazaar and W! And if that isn't proof enough, I was wearing a gold, skin-tight bathing suit and holding hands with a 20-something hunk who was staring adoringly at me.

How "old" was I? Seventy-two!

RetroAge grew out of my journey from self-loathing to self-love... a love that ultimately transcends Self. My desire to achieve life-long youth has delivered so much more than my original goal. Yes, it did turn me into a very youthful, very sexy, older beauty... but it did so much more. It transformed me into the deeply loving, courageous woman I always dreamed of becoming. I could not have asked for anything more.

"Okay" I thought, "RetroAge has proven itself. Now's my chance to share my secrets with others."

Welcome to this extraordinary adventure,

HATTIE

XIV

CHAPTER ONE
A Steam Room Vow

Odd as it may seem, my revulsion of aging began when I was five years old! That probably sounds strange, but it happens to be true. It all started when my mother took me with her to a steam bath in Brooklyn. The sight of naked, fat women terrified me.

When I was a little girl, my mother would drag me, kicking and screaming, on her weekly visits to Brighton Beach. There, in the Bath House locker room, she would undress herself and me, and lead me into the scorching steam room. We'd join a group of naked women as they happily chatted away, scrubbing their ample bodies. For them, European émigrés like my mom, these ritual sweat baths were a treat. For me, they were torture.

My mother loved being there so much that she never realized how horrible it was for me, the only child in the place. I imagine she thought it was just the heat that made me cry. To save myself, I'd crouch toward the floor, gasping for cooler air and dreaming of the frozen custard Mommy would buy for me on our way home.

When I looked up, my curious eyes were riveted to the bodies towering over me. To this day, I can see them, silhouetted in the acrid steam: lumpy flesh, flabby bellies, drooping breasts, purple veins coursing up dimpled legs… a scary sight for a young child to witness.

"If this is what ladies look like", I tearfully vowed, "I won't ever be like them. When I grow up I'll be thin and beautiful, like a model."

So, I lived for years believing that it was impossible for me to grow up to be anything like my mother or her old, fat friends. After all, I was a wild tomboy - running, climbing, playing ball, jumping rope and roller-skating. That was until I sprouted breasts, and got my period - two decidedly unwelcome events.

Much to my horror it seemed that despite my vow, I was destined to turn into one of those steam room ladies.

The future seemed bleak.

CHAPTER TWO
Overcoming Body Hatred

As a teenager, I spent countless afternoons lying on the living room couch fantasizing growing up to be glamorous like the models in the fashion magazines my mother borrowed from the library. Looking at the glossy pages, I would dream, 'Someday… someday' but I never believed that there would ever be a 'someday' for me.

My childhood was spent in a low-cost housing project in Williamsburg, Brooklyn. I always loved to dance and sing, but my parents couldn't afford lessons, so a future as a performer was out of the question. I did, however, show a talent for drawing. Because of this, my guidance counselor thought I should apply to a school that specialized in the arts. She told my parents, "Hattie is special. She should go to a special school."

By mistake, rather than requesting an application for High School of Music and Art, she sent for a form from the High School of *Performing* Arts - the one featured in the movie, "Fame." I had no idea what it was all about, but instead of a portfolio, I prepared two monologues and went for my audition. Out of about five hundred applicants, Performing Arts admitted only fifty. And miracle of miracles, Hattie from Brooklyn was one of them!

Her mistake transformed my life.

It was at Performing Arts, in a *Movement for Actors* class, that I had my first dance lesson. It felt as if I were transported to another planet. When I danced, all my self-consciousness disappeared. I felt graceful and beautiful. But it was one thing to feel ecstatic moving to music in class and quite another to experience self-love when I wasn't dancing. Traveling back home to the projects each day, those good feelings left me. On the train, I often hid my tears in a book, making believe I was reading.

I tried everything I could think of to feel better about myself. Many an afternoon found me combing through thrift shops to find glamorous, expensive-looking outfits to wear to school each day. But beautiful clothing didn't help. I felt ashamed, believing that my elegant wardrobe could never cover what was concealed underneath - thunder thighs, plushy hips and huge breasts. Even more horrifying, spider veins were already forming on my legs.

I hated my body. And I was only sixteen.

In retrospect, I admit that my self-image was distorted. At five feet, three inches tall, weighing 125 pounds, with a well-proportioned, curvaceous body, I should have been delighted. But I saw myself as dumpy and chubby. In my fantasies, I was five-ten, long-limbed and lean, small-breasted, 110 pounds, with long, straight hair. No wonder my self-image suffered. What I saw in my mirror and what I wanted to see were in no way alike.

This started a lifelong battle to be skinny.

One week I downed countless hot fudge sundaes and wore baggy pants. The next, I consumed nothing but grapefruit and black coffee and squeezed into my tightest skirts. My weight went up and down, and so did my moods. The food bingeing continued throughout my years as a student in Brooklyn College. I was elected president of the Dance Club and had to wear a leotard every day, which, of course, made me even more self-conscious. Despite my body hatred, I cultivated my dance gifts, studying and dancing as much as four hours a day.

My talents as a dancer earned me a scholarship to the Connecticut College School of Dance to study with the famed Martha Graham. There, amid an array of exquisitely toned dancers, I resolved to whip my body into shape. "Okay," I thought, "I can never be tall, but I can certainly be skinny." That decision set me off on a starvation rampage that ended up with my becoming anorexic. I can even recall eating *four* corn flakes for lunch and immediately feeling guilty that I didn't eat *three*! Such is the insanity of anorexia.

After six weeks of intensive dance studies, I returned home to Brooklyn determined to continue my quest for the perfect body. I used the bathroom scale like a Geiger counter to detect even an ounce of extra weight. But my obsession with losing weight backfired. I became ravenous and started eating whole cheesecakes, quarts of ice cream and entire pizzas! It was like being on a teeter-totter... up ten pounds, down ten pounds... fat wardrobe, thin wardrobe. There was no peace.

Thankfully, after I got married and worked as a dance teacher in New York City public schools and in my own dancing school, *The School for Creative Movement,* my overeating stopped. The satisfaction of being a wife, mother and dance teacher pushed my body hatred onto the back burner. I even stopped thinking about those steam room ladies! But twenty-five years later, when I got divorced, my disgust with my body re-surfaced. Suddenly I was forced to face being alone, creating a new career and looking for another life partner. Naked in front of new men? Now that's what I call a challenge!

As a single 48-year-old woman, doubts about my desirability began haunting me. "Am I over the hill? Have I lost my sex appeal? Will any man ever want me again? Am I doomed to be alone forever?" The psychic pain became unbearable. Once and for all, it was time for me to learn to respect myself, and to honor the gift of life.

Determined to shed my obsession with weight and aging, I began psychotherapy, hoping that it would help me overcome my body hatred and also get over my fear of aging.

And it did!

CHAPTER THREE
The Journey Begins

No longer married, and with both my children now at college, I focused on creating a new life as a single woman. With the help of my therapist, I was able to discover the true meaning of my life. Thank goodness, I ceased being tormented with questions about my desirability. Taking their place was an impassioned desire to discover and fulfill my life's mission.

I began my quest fixated on youth and beauty, but therapy helped me transform from being narcissistic and discontent to being a loving and compassionate woman. It may sound corny, but I stopped caring about the size of my thighs and concentrated on the size of my heart. This spiritual awakening inspired me to become a therapist myself. In that way, I could spend my life helping others rid themselves of the same body hatred that once plagued me.

Finally, my past pain and misery could be put to good use.

Though I wanted to get married again, like it or not, it simply wasn't happening. "Okay kid," I mused, "You have no man to lean on anymore. You're going to have to make it on your own!" At first, I resisted this idea, but there was no way to avoid the truth. I could complain and be depressed for the rest of my life, or I could create a life worth living.

My choice was clear.

Determined to achieve radiant health and unprecedented youth, I explored every technique and philosophy I could lay my hands on: chiropractors, acupuncturists, New Age healers, alternative doctors, The Forum, shiatsu, yoga, spiritual guides, hypnotism, Rolfing, reinvention, aromatherapy, Higher Balance, GOD, Abraham, Reichien therapy, homeopathy, past life regression, astrology, applied kinesiology, meditation, crystals, vitamins, herbs, massage therapy. You name it... I tried it. Each provided for me in a profound way as I shed the past Hattie.

Miracles began showing up everywhere.

Friends and clients who witnessed my metamorphosis wondered what was going on. They accused me of lying about having a facelift and urged me to reveal the name of the doctor who prescribed the youth elixir they were sure I was taking. When I replied that I didn't have surgery and the closest thing to an elixir I ever took was fresh carrot juice, they were stunned. "Hattie, please tell us your secrets" they begged.

I shared my discoveries with them... especially the importance of believing in miracles. I assured them that when you want something with all your heart and soul, and you are ready to work for it, it can be achieved. Sure enough, when they followed in my footsteps, they too achieved amazing results. The seeds of RetroAge were germinating!

I couldn't have been happier.

Now I had tangible proof that what I had done for myself wasn't a freak accident, great genes, or simply good luck. I sat myself down, retraced my steps and created a Four-Step Program that others could follow.

Enter... THE BLITZ!

CHAPTER FOUR
Blitz Baby, Blitz!

To start growing younger I had to clear away stored up possessions, clothing and memories. This meant getting rid of everything that didn't positively impact my goal of life-long youth. Clutter was keeping me stuck in the past and holding me back from fulfilling my dreams. It was time to get rid of it!

Even the neatest, most organized person has a store of items: clothing, shoes, cosmetics, books and even food that they've put aside in an "I'll need this someday" fashion.

With Blitzing,"someday" is TODAY!

A Blitz begins the process of facing things that are cluttering your life and holding you back from a youth-filled future. With it, you'll be getting rid of stuff that you may never use, and perhaps didn't even know you were holding onto - like those shoe boxes filled with spike heels that you can't walk in to save your life or the pictures and letters from your first love who broke your heart twenty years ago. And what about those fabulous "skinny" clothes that once made you feel like a million bucks? I'm pretty sure that, just like me, you've said to yourself, "When I lose weight, I'll need them again." Right! We've all fallen into *that* trap.

Every one of us has hideaways where we stash our secrets. Some people hide candy, cookies, chips, alcohol, and pints of ice cream that they eat with nobody else around. Others store letters, photographs, magazines, clothing, jewelry, china, silverware and all sorts of things they no longer need but resist getting rid of.

What are you hanging onto?

Holding onto the past - materially or emotionally - keeps you stuck in the past. Blitzing is the most powerful, proactive technique I know to help you face the future with clarity and courage.

Hattietude: Getting younger starts with clearing away the past!

ON YOUR MARK...

At first, you might resist confronting the stuff you've stashed away for years, especially when you know that you'll soon be tossing out much of it. It's not easy to face past mistakes. But when you think about it, isn't it even harder to keep on living with them? It took me years to get down to clearing out boxes of fabrics and trimmings from my years as a costume designer. Even though there was no way I would go back to that field after I became a therapist, it made me feel like I was filled with overflowing creativity. In reality, the only things that were overflowing were the cluttered boxes they were stuffed into!

With Blitzing you'll be clearing every area of your home that you've filled with unnecessary and outdated things. Don't panic; you won't have to tackle it all at once. Clearing the past happens in stages, according to your own timing, needs, and let's face it... courage.

Believe it or not, once you get over the fear that you're opening Fibber Magee's closet or Pandora's Box, you'll experience newfound freedom and lightness. Though I resisted it at first, I've come to enjoy clearing away stuff. I even created a formula to help myself decide whether to keep or to toss things. I ask myself, "If you saw this today, would you be excited to buy it?" If the answer is no... out it goes!

GET READY...GET SET... TOSS!

When you begin a Blitz, you have to set the stage:

- Put aside a block of time - at least two hours for each Blitz.
- Don the most comfortable clothes you own. A Blitz is definitely down and dirty.
- Listen to some upbeat music - Avoid Gregorian chants.
- Break out a box of super-strength jumbo garbage bags.
- Keep a box of tissues handy to dry your tears. I cried a lot on the first go-round.
- Be patient with yourself. Blitzing can be overwhelming.

It's great if a friend or two join you when you're going through your stuff. And, just in case you're afraid that they'll judge you harshly, don't worry. They won't... since they know that their closets are in the same or even worse shape than yours. Just be sure they have a sense of humor and will hold you to the spirit of the Blitz. You don't want anyone who encourages you to save 75 percent of the stuff you've just mustered up the courage to part with.

I still remember how my friends stood by patiently as I went through my prized possessions. I sobbed, recalling poignant stories of raising my children and having to leave my home after 25 years of marriage... and so on and so on. As I tearfully explained the importance of keeping a treasured piece of jewelry, or my prized, satin and lace "Marilyn Monroe" dress, they did their best to hold back their tears... but it wasn't sad tears they were holding back. They found my maudlin memories to be so funny that they began hysterically laughing. Pretty soon, I joined them, as we doubled over with laughter and filled bag after bag with things I was certain I couldn't live without.

I'm so grateful to them for sticking with me through my post-divorce Blitz. They helped me break free of my past, and move forward to a new life as a single woman. I don't think I could have done it without them. Well, even if I did, it probably would have been horrible instead of hilarious! Just follow this system and soon Blitzing will be as natural as brushing your teeth.

TIPS ON TOSSING

The best way to know if you should keep something or throw it out is to ask yourself, as I did, "If I saw it today, would I be excited to buy it?" It's shocking to realize how many things you have that you wouldn't even take if they were handed to you for free.

I always enjoy reminding myself that the stuff I'm getting rid of was bought by the woman I once was, not the one I'm becoming. That encourages me to be a whole lot less hesitant about throwing stuff out. Just because I bought something doesn't mean I have to hold onto it, wear it... or even like it! I'm a tosser. I love to get rid of stuff. But if you're a person who is concerned about being wasteful, donate the items to charity, give them to a neighbor, sell them on consignment, or eBay. But whatever you decide, GET RID OF THEM AS FAST AS YOU CAN!

The process of elimination is simple. Sort items - be they kitchen staples or clothing - into three categories:

1. **AUTOMATIC THROWAWAYS:** Things you don't have to think twice about getting rid of. Get rid of them quickly or you may talk yourself into hanging on to them even longer.

2. **POSSIBLE KEEPERS:** Items that might haunt you if you threw them away, though in your heart you know you really should part with them. With these, ask yourself if you've used them in the past six months... or if you'll need them in the upcoming six months. If the answer is no in either direction, get rid of them.

3. **DEFINITE KEEPERS:** These are the things that you truly cherish; foods that nourish your body; clothing that makes you feel sensational, items filled with precious memories.

Hopefully, very soon, DEFINITE KEEPERS will be the only category left!

A BLITZ FOR EACH STEP

With each of the four steps, you'll be doing a Blitz to clear the path to your future youth:

- STEP 1: EATING……… The kitchen
- STEP 2: ATTITUDE…… Your closets and memories
- STEP 3: SKIN CARE….. The bathroom
- STEP 4: EXERCISE…… Everywhere else

My friends often tease me, "If you're coming over, we're nailing the closets shut!" Then we laugh and start Blitzing their place together.

Now you and I - in spirit - will Blitz through your entire home step-by-step to clear a path for your dreams to be fulfilled.

Hattietude: Blitzing works like dynamite to blast you out of the past!

CHAPTER FIVE
Fighting Father Time with E.A.S.E.

It seemed like I was being super courageous when I began my mission, but underneath, I was filled with doubts. I had bought the idea that aging is a one-way destination to doom. Perhaps if being old weren't pictured as being so horrible, I might have found a way to accept it. But, thank goodness, the horror of aging set my life on a journey of transformation. I haven't regretted a moment of it.

Up through my 50's, my Anti-Aging techniques were producing great results. Then there was a shift. Father Time was chomping at the bit to take over! I didn't know what to do, but I knew that unless I became fiercely determined to reverse this seemingly inevitable decline, all would be lost.

Unacceptable!

My answer came in a very unexpected way. Here's the story:

One day in 1988, at fifty-two, I spotted a notice in the newspaper about an Over-50 Bathing Suit Beauty Contest at the famed Roseland Ballroom. I decided to enter. Tucking my sexiest swimsuit into my bag, off I went to Roseland.

I arrived early and began dancing with one of the "regulars." When people saw me dance, they urged me on, "You're gonna win. We'll see to that!" Sure enough, when I paraded in front of the judges, I could hear them clapping and wildly cheering behind me.

I won first prize!

I never planned to be a beauty queen. I was as shocked at winning as I was at how people were inspired by me. Everyone was so supportive and complimentary, especially when they told me that seeing me "strut my stuff" in a scanty suit encouraged them to be more confident themselves. The most fascinating part of winning was that while they were assuring me that I had given *them* courage and hope, I was thinking that *they* were giving *me* courage and hope.

At 9:00am the next morning, without feeling the least bit self-conscious, I stepped onto the set of the Regis & Kathie Lee Show in the same swimsuit I'd worn at Roseland the night before. Regis jumped up, put his hand on his forehead and pretended he was going to faint:

"OmiGod! Hattie! Many women your age would be afraid to appear on television in a bathing suit." Then, he looked out at the audience and praised me warmly. "Once in a while you meet someone who's not afraid to take chances... who goes out there and does what she has to do. God bless you, you look fabulous. There she is - an inspiration to all of America." I will never forget Regis' encouraging words.

Adding to that, the *New York Daily News* ran a huge photo of me with the headline "Golden Boldie" and raved, "Wiener makes Cher look like John Candy on a bad day."

The excitement, publicity and respect from winning the contest revealed something about myself that I had never owned up to before... that my role in life was to inspire others. This was the answer I was looking for. From then on, I was going to spend my life transforming both the *perception* and the *experience* of aging for people everywhere. Helping others to face their aging battles would force me to be relentless in discovering and creating new ways to achieve lifetime youth and beauty.

I felt so fortunate that this was revealed to me. It was to be the mission worthy of a lifetime that I had prayed for.

To begin with, I wanted to understand America's obsession with youth and beauty. The information we've been fed since childhood has ingrained horrible images of what it means to be old. Adding to that, each day we see evidence of individuals whose aging reinforces these images – halting gait, hunching over, wheelchairs, walkers, dull, lifeless skin, flaccid musculature, diminished energy, false teeth, dowdy clothing, dry, wrinkled skin, dull eyes, memory loss... and those are just the obvious ones.

This is what I would be up against if I were going to turn around the awful way in which aging is viewed in our culture. I knew that convincing others that there is beauty and youth at every age would be a huge challenge. I was thrilled to take it on. With newfound confidence, I set out to create a program that others could follow so Father Time couldn't come a knockin' at their doors to claim them.

I retraced the steps in my own youth-seeking journey, and distilled my method into the Four Step RetroAge Program. Then I noticed a welcome surprise. After I wrote the steps down, I noticed that if I ordered them in a special way, they spelled **EASE.**

THE 4 STEP RETROAGE E.A.S.E. PROGRAM

- **E = Eating**
- **A = Attitude**
- **S = Skin Care...and the final**
- **E = Exercise!**

To launch my new concept, I trademarked and registered the word "RetroAge." As in the Bible, "In the beginning was the word." This new word would become the focus of my life. I invite you to step forth with me and create a life of abundant energy, creativity, beauty and sexuality - all the attributes of youth that we fear will leave us as we age. With RetroAge, they don't have to.

Hattietude: Your first youth is a gift from Nature.
Your life-long youth is a gift from yourself!

CHAPTER SIX
STEP 1...Eating

Here is your first step in the Four Step E.A.S.E. Program. Over the years, I've tried virtually every weight-loss diet ever invented. With one, I ate so much pineapple I felt like a human piña colada. With another, all I could have were liquids. With most of them, the pounds would drop away at first, then they'd return, leaving me frustrated and disappointed. After testing a slew of weight loss styles, I discovered one that I've been following for years – FOOD COMBINING.

THERE IS NO WAY TO CREATE YOUTH

WITHOUT GIVING YOUR BODY

ABUNDANT NUTRIENTS EVERY SINGLE DAY

If the word "healthy" elicits images of unappetizing, bland, tasteless, "eat it because it's good for you" food, don't worry. With RetroAge Eating you won't be sentenced to a life of munching sawdusty grains, gritty glop, and tasteless concoctions.

So read on to learn how to master FOOD COMBINING; a relatively unknown way of eating that guarantees a slender, healthy, appealing body for a lifetime.

FOOD COMBINING...WAY TO GO

When I studied how my body reacted to different ways of eating, I realized that the only way I could stay healthy and thin was to practice a system that I had once read about - FOOD COMBINING. As long as I stuck to this regime, my weight stayed low and my energy stayed high. Any time I strayed, I began to feel and look awful. Then, getting back on track, my skin became radiant again, my eyes bright, my digestion good. In fact, people would tell me that I glowed.

You too can have these same results.

For me, the health benefits of FOOD COMBINING were so powerful that I recommended to my clients that they follow it too. Prior to introducing this unique style of eating, I simply focused on the nutritive value of food, adhering to the common belief that combining complex carbs, protein, and simple carbs *at each meal* make for balanced nutrition.

"Why shouldn't we combine animal proteins and complex carbs at the same meal?" my clients would ask. It bothered me not to be able to give them an answer other than to assure them that it works. There was some biochemical reason behind it, but I hadn't the foggiest notion what it was. Then one day while discussing RetroAge Eating with a client he remarked, "This sounds a lot like how my mother cooked for me when I was a kid. In fact, I still have her cookbook somewhere. I'll find it and bring it to you."

He found the book and brought it to me at his very next session.

The book, "*The Official Cook Book of the Hay System*" by Esther L. Smith, with an introduction by William Howard Hay, M.D. is long out of print. In fact, it was published in August of 1934, before I was even born! Much to my surprise it had all the answers I was searching for.

As Dr. Hay wrote in the introduction to the eleventh printing (October 1940):

"Foods are of vastly different sorts, also as regards to the digestive requirements, some being digested largely in one part of the digestive tract while others digest in a different part, and the body modifies the digestive juices to suit the tasks at hand at the time.

Basically, foods are carbohydrates or proteins, each with vastly different digestive requirements, so different that they are even digested in separate parts of the system. Carbohydrates: cereals, potatoes, corn, pumpkins and dry fruits like dates and raisins start digesting in the mouth, where ptyalin in the saliva splits them into dextrose (sugars), they then pass through the acidic stomach to continue the process in the alkaline medium found in the intestines. Animal Proteins: meats, seafood and cheese need the strong gastric juices, pepsin and hydrochloric acid, found in the stomach to release their nutrients.

If carbohydrates and proteins are in the stomach at the same time, the stomach acid starts the fermentation process on the carbohydrates, which interferes with the digestion of the proteins. The result is chaos… fermentation, gas, acidosis…illness in one form or other."

Finally…a clear explanation!

To help you master the principles of FOOD COMBINING, I've stripped it down to its two elemental categories:

GROUP 1:

STARCHY COMPLEX CARBOHYDRATES AND

VEGETABLE PROTEINS

GROUP 2:

ANIMAL PROTEINS

REMEMBER THE RULE...

YOU MUST NEVER EAT FOODS FROM GROUP 1

WITH FOODS FROM GROUP 2 IN THE SAME MEAL

GROUP 1

COMPLEX CARBS AND VEGETABLE PROTEINS

Rice, wheat, barley and other grains, teff, quinoa, rice, wild rice, beans and peas, potatoes, winter squashes, corn, bread, pasta, tofu, tempeh, chips, pretzels, cereals, raw or roasted nuts, seeds and nut butters.

RULE: *When you eat complex carbs, you can eat only vegetables, cooked or raw, including salad with them.*
REMEMBER: *Absolutely no animal protein, not even a splash of grated cheese, sour cream, milk, cream or yogurt.*

GROUP 2

ANIMAL PROTEINS

Chicken, turkey, all fowl, fish, beef, pork, veal, eggs, milk, cheese, yogurt and all milk products (canned, bottled and fresh).

RULE: *When you eat animal protein, you can only eat vegetables, cooked or raw, including salad with them.*

**DON'T WORRY, YOU WON'T HAVE TO MAKE DRASTIC
CHANGES ALL AT ONCE
RETROAGE EATING HAPPENS IN STAGES**

NO CUISINE USES FOOD COMBINING...PUZZLING!

What's so baffling to me is that these FOOD COMBINING concepts go against *everything* you ever learned about eating. Adding to that, there's hardly even one cuisine from any culture that follows these principles. (Israeli, Arabic and Vegetarian come close). For example: chicken and rice, spaghetti and meatballs, chili con carne, pizza, franks and beans, dumplings, ham and eggs, Irish stew, sushi, burgers and fries... and, alas, just about every conceivable sandwich.

This really puzzles me. But puzzling or not, FOOD COMBINING WORKS!

THE SKINNY ON FATS

I'm definitely not in the NO FAT or even the LOW FAT camps. I believe that the body needs fat. But though I approve of eating fats, not all fats are good for you. Certain ones are no-no's, like saturated animal fats and Trans fats. They've been implicated as causes of cancer and heart attacks.

No matter what you've heard, **all plant oils contain 0% cholesterol.** Also, natural fats from nuts, avocados and vegetables aren't fattening. If advertisements have given you the mistaken impression that plant fats are unhealthy, it's time to give up that faulty concept. In fact, even saturated fats from plant sources are fabulous for your health and for keeping you young and sexy.

ABOUT RETROAGE EATING

1. *Don't weigh yourself more than once every few days. The fit of your clothing is a better indicator than your scale.*

2. *It's how you feel and look that's important, not the numbers.*

3. *Don't think of this as a diet. Think of it as a new way of eating for the rest of your life.*

4. *Never skip meals to make up for overeating, or to lose weight or inches quickly. Drastically cutting food intake slows down metabolism and makes you hungrier.*

5. *Don't be ashamed to admit to yourself (and others) what you're actually eating. Feeling guilty won't help you lose weight. It's self-respect and self-discipline that'll keep you thin, healthy and youthful.*

6. *When you begin, be prepared to be overly involved with food and eating. Your entire relationship to food will be challenged as you adopt this new style of eating.*

7. *Locate restaurants that serve delicious, healthy food. This will make it easier for you to eat right when dining out.*

8. *Eat foods as close to their pure, unprocessed, unrefined form as possible.*

9. *Buy as many organically grown foods as your budget allows. Not only is this great for you, it supports chemical-free, naturally composted farming, which is good for the environment.*

10. *Eat until you're satisfied. If you don't, you risk triggering a tailspin of bad eating.*

Remember the Hattietude:
Deprivation Backfires.
Satisfaction Inspires!

"YOUTHFOODS™" AND "AVOIDS"

To help you define which foods create radiant health, and which ones destroy your body's health, I've created two categories:

"YOUTHFOODS™" and "AVOIDS"

The "**YOUTHFOODS™**" are all foods and beverages that enhance your health and allow your body to look and feel wonderful at every age. They encourage regeneration and insure a strong immune system.

The "**AVOIDS**" are commonly eaten foods that not only aren't healthy, they're filled with chemicals and toxins that damage your body: sugared cereals; hot dogs and other processed meats; artificial sweeteners; artificial anything; white bread; white rice and pasta; cookies; candies; cakes; ice cream; frozen, canned and bottled sugary juices.

My rule of thumb: "The closer the food is to its natural state, the better it is for keeping you healthy and YOUNG!"

Over the course of about 10 years, I've systematically eliminated all **AVOIDS** from my diet, except for an occasional slip-up. Believe me, it wasn't easy, and it still isn't! From time to time, when I do go off track, I get back to RetroAge Eating as soon as I can. Strange, but true – no sooner do I eat even one **AVOID,** than I begin *craving* them like an addict. It's downhill after that, until I discipline myself to cut it out, and get back to my RetroAge Eating regime.

I've learned that each time I marshal the discipline to say no to something unhealthy, a delicious, satisfying alternative shows up. Try this yourself. Pretty soon you'll discover fabulous new foods, beverages, herbs, spices... and restaurants!

Hattietude: Saying no opens you to life-transforming yeses!

THE "WRITE IT DOWN" YOUTHFOOD PROGRAM

Before you can transform your style of eating, you have to become aware of what you're currently eating. That's where your EATING DIARY comes in. With it, you'll be filling in a log of *everything* you eat and drink for seven days.

One thing that's different about this diary is that I've included a REASONS FOR EATING column. Not only will you be listing your foods and beverages, you'll be adding your *reasons*. Writing down the *whys* along with the *whats* will help define your emotional/addictive cravings. We all have those.

Here's how your 7-day EATING DIARY works:

As soon as you eat or drink something - a meal, a snack, a cup of coffee or tea, a soda, anything - *immediately* note the *day, time, what, how much,* and the *reason*. Record *everything* and resist the temptation to edit your entries. Tell the truth, even if it's embarrassing - it'll help you in the long run.

> BEWARE! PRACTICALLY EVERY FOOD OR BEVERAGE
> ADVERTISED ON TV IS AT BEST, EMPTY
> ...AND AT WORST, TOXIC
> READ THE LABELS AND YOU'LL SEE WHAT I MEAN

GIVE UP GUILT!

Don't indulge in guilt. It'll only slow you down. If you ate it or drank it, write it down. Listing what you're eating isn't meant to make you judge yourself harshly, or feel guilty or ashamed. Everyone overeats from time to time, even disciplined dancers and athletes. Even me!

I remember the day that a toned, slender dancer came to my studio to take classes. No sooner did she enter the studio than I felt jealous, followed by guilt over being jealous. I imagined that she had perfect discipline... not my strong point. After class when we were changing back into our street clothes, she whipped out a huge chocolate bar, and ate the whole thing. She'll never know how happy that made me!

On the next page is a blank EATING DIARY form for you to fill out. It's a good idea to photocopy a week's worth of blank charts so you can carry a page with you during the day. Then you won't have to rely on your memory when you get home.

At the end of each day, read over your EATING DIARY. **Circle** all the **YOUTH FOODS** and **cross out** all the **AVOIDS.** Do this every day, tallying your circles and crosses to track your progress. You'll know you're getting the hang of it when each day shows fewer and fewer **AVOIDS** and more and more **YOUTHFOODS**™ from the previous day.

Hattietude: Both shame and blame maim!

EATING DIARY

DATE_____

WHAT EATEN & AMOUNT	TIME	REASON Emotions and circumstances

DAILY TALLY:

Circled *YOUTHFOODS*™*:*_____   Crossed out *AVOIDS:*_____

PUTTING IT ALL TOGETHER

I had no trouble understanding the principles of FOOD COMBINING after reading Dr. Hay's explanation. But incorporating them into my life was another story. Who wants to have to keep separating the two food groups? It took plenty of determination to keep me from slipping back to my former eating style. Old habits hang on, especially when everyone around you is eating the "normal" way, and looking at you like you're some sort of kook.

Well, when you eat this way, you'll join me in being a "kook" - a fit, healthy, sexy one!

I'd like to give you a guarantee that with this plan you will *never* eat poorly again. I can't. The fact is that you probably will. But I *can* guarantee that when you do veer off course, resuming RetroAge Eating will bring your body and weight back into balance.

There's no getting around it. For life-long youth, everything you eat and drink must be healthy! Okay, perhaps not everything, but most of it.

I must confess that there are times when my old cravings crop up. Nope... they haven't completely disappeared. Ice cream is my personal nemesis. What's interesting is that each time I indulge in a pint (or two) of ice cream, I go into a tailspin of bad eating, gain weight, get tired, exercise less, and end up even hungrier. Then I feel so sluggish that the only exercise I do is racing back and forth to the freezer to polish off that haunting pint of ice cream that's beckoning me!

You may have noticed that I haven't said a word about counting calories, computing fat grams or even portion sizes. This doesn't mean that I'm not concerned about being overweight. I am. But with RetroAge Eating and FOOD COMBINING your body finds its own balance, and you stay in tip-top shape.

Hattietude: Stick to Food Combining and the weight won't stick to you!

WHAT TO DO IN RESTAURANTS

Who hasn't rationalized overeating in a restaurant with: "I have no control over what they serve, so I might as well give up and enjoy myself." Here are some ways to get around this rationale so that you can stick to the program and still enjoy a night out:

- Ask the waiter to take away that tempting basket of white rolls and breadsticks and the little dish of butter. If you would like something to munch on while waiting for your meal, request a bowl of crudités, or order a glass of wine. YES, RetroAge Eating includes moderate drinking.

- When you're checking out the menu, make a fast calculation! If you plan to order a meal with animal protein, ask your waiter to substitute veggies or salad for the rice, potatoes or pasta. Also avoid eating the bread or bread sticks, even if they're made of nutritious whole grains. Even though they may be healthy, they're made of flour - a starchy carbohydrate.

- And, whenever you can, skip dessert... and those tempting mints near the exit.

Hattietude: New habits make for new bodies!

DON'T THINK OF RETROAGE EATING AS A DIET...
IT'S A NEW MODE OF EATING TO KEEP YOU YOUTHFUL AND
FIT... FOR LIFE!

AN APPLE A DAY ... AND THEN SOME

The American Cancer Society recommends that you have five fresh vegetables and fruits each day. Follow their advice, but make sure that several are *raw*. Raw food insures that your body receives the enzymes necessary for efficient digestion. Because much of the food we eat is cooked, which destroys enzymes, it's a good idea to eat something raw at every meal.

I love *freshly squeezed* vegetable and fruit juices. They deliver a powerful shot of valuable nutrition and provide a welcome energy boost. Note that I stipulated *freshly squeezed*, so go for FRESH and RAW. Bottled juices are usually pasteurized.

ALTERING YOUR FOOD CONSCIOUSNESS

When I began eating the RetroAge way, I cut back on red meats for health reasons. I soon felt "cleaner" and more energized. I continued to eat poultry and seafood because they were lighter and less fatty than meat and also easier to digest. Then, a friend gave me a copy of John Robbin's revealing book, "*Diet for a New America.*"

Reading his graphic descriptions of the brutalization of animals made me change my personal style of eating, though I didn't become 100 percent vegan, as he recommends. I eliminated all meat from animals that didn't eat meat themselves, reasoning, "If they're vegetarians, I don't want to eat them." Giving up foods that I formerly enjoyed was hard, but thinking about the treatment of the animals helped me discipline myself, even though I was, and still am, tempted. On the other hand, since fish eat each other, I feel fine about eating those non-vegetarians!

I have found the benefits of not eating meat to be so amazing that I came very close to recommending that RetroAge Eating be vegetarian. But I won't. Vegetarianism is an extremely complex and emotionally charged issue. I don't feel right about preaching that everyone should eliminate animals from their diet, especially since it took me decades to do that for myself.

However, if you choose to eat meat and poultry, I strongly recommend that they be organically raised. In that way you may not be saving the animals, but you'll be saving yourself from the hormones, antibiotics and drugs that "conventional" farmers routinely use.

Also, whenever you can, purchase dairy products and eggs that are organically raised…or at least those whose packaging specifies that no hormones or antibiotics are used. The negative effects from animal products tend to be more toxic than those from vegetables and fruits.

RETROAGE EATING

Don't become obsessed with how much you eat, or with calorie counting. Proper weight control depends on feeling satisfied and not walking around hungry. It takes time to master FOOD COMBINING… so don't be angry with yourself for occasional binges. A healthy body can handle them.

KITCHEN BLITZ

Now, with all the nuts and bolts of RetroAge Eating out of the way, it's time to begin your first kitchen Blitz. Notice I said *first*. As you become more committed to RetroAging, you'll find yourself Blitzing at regular intervals.

Now, we're going to get rid of everything that doesn't aid you in achieving youth. It's time to get out those garbage bags, put on your sweats and toss all those "can't live withouts" that are cluttering your kitchen...and your life.

Many times I've had a tug-of-war with a client over a box of macaroni or a bottle of ketchup. They'd rather use it up, concerned about wasting a couple of dollars. Worrying about money in these instances is definitely penny wise and age foolish.

After you've completed your Blitz, congratulate yourself... you've taken the first cut at the **AVOIDS** in your kitchen. The shock of clearing out cupboard shelves laden with macaroni and cheese and assorted snacks and a fridge filled with cans of soda, bacon and prepared dinners can traumatize even the staunchest youth-seeker.

It may be thrilling to see all that clear space. But it could also have the opposite effect. Since you're giving up familiar ways of shopping, cooking and eating, you might feel anxious. That's a natural reaction. It takes time for Blitzing to become a welcome habit... and even more time for it to become FUN! I've come to love Blitzing. It always gets me going in a new direction.

After having tossed so much stuff you may find yourself facing a lot of space begging to be filled. Don't rush out and fill them up again until you're sure you'll be restocking them with **YOUTHFOODS** that nourish your body and contribute to a new, younger you.

CHAPTER SEVEN
STEP 2...Attitude

The mind is an awesome force. When it delivers destructive images, they are well on their way to becoming true. Thankfully, the reverse is equally true. You can reprogram your thinking and reverse the negative effects of aging as soon as they show up. At first, you may believe as I once did, that it isn't possible to reverse aging. RetroAge teaches you that this is not so. The body, mind and spirit are blessed with an infinite capacity to transform and regenerate.

While all four steps of RetroAge are important, **ATTITUDE** was the most confronting one for me. I was coming from a very negative point of view about aging. To put it simply, I hated it! It doesn't take much to know that being repulsed by something hampers the chances of overcoming it. My work was cut out for me.

As a therapist, I knew that the best way to make any change is to affirm and accept what exists. After that, it becomes easier to move towards the desired goal. I was faced with a dilemma - how could I affirm or accept aging when it repulsed me? Repulsed? Yes, repulsed. Admittedly a harsh word, but one that unfortunately, accurately described my feelings.

Since I had decided to spend my life finding ways to achieve life-long youth, I took on the challenge of tracing the source of my personal revulsion. It was time to get to the root of this hatred and to turn it around.

From childhood on, we're programmed to believe that aging is a one-way ticket to doom. For sure, most of the dread comes from society and the media. It doesn't help that we are bombarded daily with TV ads featuring young people jumping up and down with boundless energy with nary a bag, sag or wrinkle in sight. And then there are the impeccably made-up women urging us to buy their wrinkle removing crèmes so that we too can achieve the lineless, smiling face of youth.

All this reinforces the idea that aging is to be avoided *at all cost.* All it takes is to use this or that product, or doctor or whatever. Yes, "at all cost"... and the "cost" can be very high, both financially and spiritually.

I wish it were simply a question of the media feeding us these distortions. But the problem lies much deeper than that. It seems that almost everyone in America hates aging. Some readily admit it, some don't, but most people feel this way, especially women. Distorted or not, the truth is that many of my friends and clients view the prospect of aging as one of the most horrible scenarios they could conjure up.

Since I felt that way too, I forced myself to work even harder to maintain a youthful appearance. In fact, on the surface it looked like I had the issue of aging solved. I was fit, toned, and I looked decades younger than my age. People even thought that I was immune to the effects of time. Nothing could have been further from the truth. Though I religiously followed 3 of the 4 steps of my program, the one step I had trouble mastering was this second step - **ATTITUDE.**

Hardly a day would pass when I didn't hear insults from inside my head, "You're too old to be sexy. Give it up." "You look ridiculous in that outfit. It's for a much younger woman." "Why would a young guy want to sleep with you when there are so many gorgeous young women out there?" "Face it... your looks are gone, and you're gonna keep getting uglier." "Everyone's looking at you and laughing." Now, if these awful thoughts are running through *my* brain, I can only imagine what terrible things are running through other people's minds.

I had positioned myself as a spokesperson for Exquisite Aging, speaking and writing about how our society condemns aging, and yet, I could have given them a run for the money. There I was, my life dedicated to inspiring others to honor themselves at every age, and yet holding onto the very feelings I was battling. I felt like a hypocrite. It was time to conquer my self-sabotage.

I decided to confront my demoralizing thoughts about aging head-on by writing them down. I was literally going to face the enemy. After seeing my complaints in black and white, I set out to create powerful, positive statements to counter the negativity that was controlling my life. I dubbed these positive statements **RETROAGERS.**

At the beginning, your negative feelings might prevail. But, pretty soon you'll become skilled at reversing the entrenched **DESTRUCTIVE AGING THOUGHTS,** replacing them with positive, inspiring **RETROAGERS.** Don't worry if you feel disgusted, discouraged or even depressed. It takes time to change destructive ways of thinking.

ALTERING NEGATIVE AGING ATTITUDES

DESTRUCTIVE AGING THOUGHTS	RETROAGERS
I'd better be careful. If I'm not, I'll fall and break my bones and end up in a wheelchair and never be able to dance again.	I'm not going to overprotect myself. Children fall all the time, and they're fine. I love to be active, so I won't let fear of falling hold me back.
I'll probably get lazy and not want to work out.	I love feeling and looking fit so nothing will stop me from going to my health club whether I'm in the mood or not.
I'll probably start getting forgetful and slow-witted as I age.	I intend to keep challenging my mind with new ideas, projects, travel, and friends.
My sex drive will probably fade away.	I'll find ways to be sexy always… all ways.
I'd better become more conservative in my style or people will think I'm weird.	I really don't care what people think about me. I love being authentic, and I've become much braver now that I'm older.

It's impossible to keep starting over and getting braver and more youthful with each passing year.	I'm unstoppable. Now that I have a few years behind me, I have the wisdom and the time to do all those things I dreamed of as a youth.
I'll probably have to reign in my desire for younger men and sex. After all who will want me when I'm old?	No way am I going to pull back on my desire for love, and lovers. There are plenty of men who desire older women. They'll desire me!
I can't fight Mother Nature.	Fighting Mother Nature is good exercise.
After forty, you're over the hill.	I'll keep climbing and never be over the hill.
You can't teach an old dog new tricks.	I'm not an old dog. What a demeaning image!
The world only wants to see and hear young people. Old people are passé.	The world needs to learn from older people... the young need us to inspire and guide them.
Being old is a disgusting punishment.	Aging is a glorious adventure, if I handle it right!

Hattietude: Discontent is the first step to discovery!

CREATIVE SELF-DISGUST!

I made up the term "Creative Self Disgust" to sweeten and lighten the pervasive negative self-judgments we all have coming from inside our heads. Acknowledging our fears and hates and then converting them into constructive, positive action transforms them from being discouraging downers to creative motivators. Now that's a great example of energy conversion!

What I'm recommending it that you avoid buying into believing that you will become a victim of negativity, whether it's coming from yourself, or from the media. It's okay to feel lousy sometimes...who doesn't? Sure, feeling lousy can depress and paralyze you. But it can also provide the fire in your belly that gets you moving in the right direction.

ABOUT ATTITUDE

- *Don't expect your attitudes toward aging – and yourself – to change overnight.*
- *Backslides will discourage you. They're to be expected. Keep working in the face of them.*
- *Don't ever think you're too old for really dramatic changes.*
- *Consider that what you think about aging is based on your past history, and the past history of humanity (in our culture). It may be entirely off the mark and ready for major revision – culturally and personally.*
- *Be ready to give up old concepts, habits and possessions.*
- *Also be prepared to get depressed, disgusted, and discouraged! Remember that the first step to transformation is discontent and disgust with what already exists. I call this "Creative Self-Disgust".*
- *BELIEVE IN MIRACLES!*

LEARNING FROM CHILDREN

Sometimes I look into the eyes of elderly people and imagine seeing the child they once were. I wonder what happened to turn them into old people. What became of the bubbly spirit, the wildness, the playfulness, the optimism and the joy? It's a question I often ask myself.

I have been very fortunate. My background as a teacher of dance to children has allowed me to maintain the spirit of youth. For over fifteen years, I taught creative dance to several hundred pre-schoolers. The memories of my students as they ran, jumped, fell, giggled and jostled one another remain with me to this day. I played and laughed with them … and they taught me one of the greatest lessons of my life:

IT ALL HAS TO DO WITH SPIRIT... AND

SPIRIT IS AGELESS

Because of this connection to spirit, certain physical aspects of aging didn't feel as daunting to me as I would have expected. Don't get me wrong. I wasn't giving up on my appearance. Beauty and glamour have always been important to me, but my joie de vivre always triumphed over a sag here and a wrinkle there.

I had no idea of the power of spirit until I experienced a deep shift in my soul with RetroAge. The prospect of aging ceased to terrify me. I stopped hating the aging process and began to take aging into my own hands with the enthusiasm of a child. Challenges became opportunities.

The shift happened on the inside, but the transformation was apparent on the outside. I was visibly looking younger. My stamina soared. I became stronger, more creative, courageous and lighter. Not only did I lose weight, I lost the heavy burden of worry, fear and envy as well. I no longer dressed, moved, behaved or thought like the stereotypical older woman. Whenever I detected any "old lady" behavior, I consciously put in an immediate correction. Sure, as we age, we don't have precisely the same skin or muscle tone we once had. But that doesn't have to stop us from growing more youthful each day. True youth is vibrancy, energy, courage, joyfulness and openness – the delightful child-like attributes we can maintain at every age.

When people ask, "How long does it take to RetroAge?"

My answer - "Your whole life... if you're lucky!"

HATTIETUDES™ BUILD HAPPINESS

Poking fun at our flaws and foibles is a valuable tool in your RetroAge arsenal. What could be more liberating than facing your own demons and neutralizing them? Even better, you can learn to laugh at them. However, we cannot overlook the fact that life is full of experiences that sadden us, shock us, and bring us to our knees.

We often need inspiration to keep our spirits up. I have created **Hattietudes** to provide positive, life-affirming messages for you to reach for whenever you feel low or discouraged. It is my hope that these **Hattietudes** act as "booster shots" to infuse your life with optimism, faith and joy.

Hattietude: The opposite of old isn't young...it's NEW!

20 HATTIETUDES TO INSPIRE YOU TO RETROAGE

1. *Age is not the reason... it's the excuse!*
2. *Never forget the YOU in Youth!*
3. *Impossible = I'm Possible!*
4. *Life gets harder, but you get smarter!*
5. *The hands of time are yours. Take aging into your own hands!*
6. *Don't let gravity get you down!*
7. *Fighting Mother Nature is good exercise!*
8. *Love is contagious. Go out and catch some!*
9. *Your first youth is a gift from nature; your life-long youth is a gift from yourself!*
10. *Convert envy into inspiration and you'll never run out of fuel!*
11. *Blame and shame maim!*
12. *Age doesn't make you forget... it teaches you what's important to remember!*
13. *Bless every rejection. It takes hundreds of them to get one good yes!*
14. *Wrinkles don't make you old. Babies have plenty of them!*
15. *Suffering is an option you don't have to pick up!*
16. *Where there's a will there's a won't. Respect the negative!*
17. *Never give up on your dreams. They keep you awake!*
18. *If it's been done, you can do it. If it hasn't, you can be the first!*
19. *Hate aging and it'll hate you back. Love it and it'll love you back!*
20. *Youth isn't wasted on the young – or on anyone else!*

My clients have shared some of their attitude shifts so that I can pass them along to you.

- "I can now treat myself exquisitely, no matter how others have treated me and how I have treated myself in the past."
- "I will find my own personal style of experiencing aging so that I am excited at what the future holds."
- "I can change my negative habits of behavior and thought into positive, life-affirming actions."
- "It is a privilege to share myself with others."
- "I am truly grateful to be alive... at any age."

Hattietude: Even if you haven't reached all your goals... you've still reached!

TIME TO BLITZ AGAIN!

With this Blitz, you'll be ridding your home of even more clutter. It's great to periodically toss things that you neither need nor use. Then you can soar into the future unencumbered by relics of the past. Go into your attic, storage space or wherever you have pile-ups, collections and God knows what else. Decide if you really want to hold onto the cribs and high chairs that your now-grown children used; the dresses you or your kids wore to proms decades ago; old suits; broken radios and appliances you never repaired. If these things don't serve a positive purpose in your life, get rid of them... *fast!*

Remember that by Blitzing stuff you're holding onto, you'll also be shedding your former self-image. Of course, I'm not telling you to throw everything but the hangers away. Just make sure you only keep things you love. And to top it off, when you've gotten rid of a pile of outdated clothing, you can treat yourself to a shopping spree for a flattering, updated wardrobe. You'll deserve one after all the tossing!

When I first restyled my own look, I tried an experiment: I asked a twenty-year-old salesclerk at a trendy SoHo shop to choose a dress for me. She brought out a sexy backless white cotton outfit from Italy that I was sure was wrong for me. But I reminded myself that this was only an experiment.

When I parted the dressing room curtains and walked into the store, I was greeted with "oohs" and "ahs" from other customers. A month later, I wore this same ensemble on national TV. And just in case you're wondering what's happened to that prize outfit, it's been replaced by a slinky black Norma Kamali minidress... the one I wore on the Howard Stern Show 10 years later - without a bra!

Hattietude: Clearing the past keeps you present in the present!

CHAPTER EIGHT
STEP 3...Skin Care

It's often remarked that children have beautiful skin and as we age, we lose this attribute. We are taught to believe that this is a logical progression, and that there's nothing to be done about it. Well, I find this unacceptable...and hope you do too. Regardless of what you've been told, beauty is never just skin deep. I tell my clients that true beauty radiates from within. We all posses it, but first we must claim it by giving ourselves the respect and care we deserve.

Of the four steps of RetroAge, **SKIN CARE**, the S, in the E.A.S.E. Program is my personal favorite. For as many years as I can remember, I've taken great care of my skin, treating myself to luxurious massages and using the finest aromatherapy oils and crèmes I could find.

There is no way to be youthful without making sure that your skin is radiantly healthy. Exquisite skin is one of our most prized possessions. When your skin is beautiful, you feel beautiful. When was the last time someone said your skin was as soft as a baby's bottom? Recently, I hope, but I suspect that's not likely. With RetroAge Skin Care you will restore your body to silken smoothness – perhaps not precisely the aforementioned baby's bottom, but lovely nevertheless.

It doesn't matter what condition it's in to begin with. I promise you that consistent care will produce consistent results. Don't give up – be relentless! It's worth it. Be forewarned... many of my RetroAge Skin Care recommendations will probably seem weird at first, especially since you've always been told to treat your skin with kid gloves. My style leans more to boxing gloves!

Even my most dedicated clients were hesitant to try my techniques at first. Nobody had ever told them to brush their face with a dry brush before. Hair, yes, but face? "Are you nuts?" they'd say. "Stretch and pull my skin? No way," they protested. "It'll make my face sag! I'll need a facelift!" Once they got over their initial shock, they never looked back. Several even decided against having the facelifts and eyelifts they were planning. Thank God.

THE SKIN IS A FABULOUS INDICATOR OF HEALTH

Everything that's wrong with your health will ultimately show up on your skin. As the body's largest organ, it is a strong indicator of your general well-being.

THE BIG THREE OF SKIN CARE

Let's go over three basic components of the RetroAge Skin Care Program:

- **Exfoliation**
- **Circulation**
- **Hydration**

First, there's **Exfoliation,** the sloughing off of dead cells. Children's bodies naturally shed skin cells. Aging, sun exposure and other stresses cause this process to slow down markedly, leaving you with dry, wrinkly skin. Mother Nature, like any mother, gets too busy to take care of you, so you'll have to exfoliate your entire body yourself. It might start out feeling like a chore. It ends up feeling delicious.

Here's my first piece of "weird" advice:

Just as a carpenter sands a piece of wood, I recommend that you rub your body vigorously with rough cloths, stiff bristle brushes, pumice stones, loofahs, gritty scrubs and soaps. Yes, to have great skin, you've got to exfoliate your dry, dead skin while showering or bathing. Now, of course, you don't want to draw blood… but be as rough as you can be, while being careful not to break skin.

This brisk removal of dead cells unclogs pores and creates smooth, blemish-free skin. Pretty soon you'll see your brown spots get lighter, imperfections will smooth away along with calluses and other assorted "crusties" that time has deposited on your body.

Hattietude: You've got to get rough to get smooth!

DRY BRUSHING… THE SECRET TO GORGEOUS SKIN

The wet exfoliation I described above should be done daily when you shower or bathe. Dry brushing, on the other hand, is much more forceful and should be done about once a week. If your skin is sensitive, adjust the frequency and forcefulness of both wet and dry brushing to avoid irritation.

The first dry brush I ever used was a common, everyday natural bristle scrub brush like one you'd use on the floor. I picked it up in the supermarket for less than $3. Soon I had all of my clients scrubbing away. After a few weeks one regular client who had been seeing great results reported that, to her horror, she returned home to find her housekeeper happily scrubbing away on her bathroom floor with her brush.

So, that's a good reason to buy two brushes and hide one. Sorry to say that within the last few years, supermarkets have replaced the natural bristle brushes with nylon ones. Under no circumstances should you use those.

Natural or Nuthin'!

Luckily, I stumbled upon a hardware store that still stocks them. I hope you do too. If not, there are some good mitts and brushes in your local drug and health food stores. Buy the stiffest natural fiber ones you can find.

Remember to scrub and oil your elbows. Wrinkly, dry elbows are a tell tale sign of aging. I've even used fine-grain sandpaper to smooth them out. Also make sure that your hands and feet are silky and soft. Dry, dead cuticles and calluses, especially on the feet, are not only old-looking, they are also potentially painful. Anyone who's had sore feet knows what I mean: It's like having a toothache all over your body.

The second factor is **Circulation:** the flow of blood through the veins, arteries and capillaries. That's how we get nutrients and oxygen to our cells, and get rid of impurities, wastes and toxins. Both brushing and massage enhance circulation.

THE HEALING POWER OF TOUCH

I believe we don't fully acknowledge the healing power of touch. Babies who are not held have been known to die. One can only imagine the effect the absence of touch has on adults. I haven't seen any statistics on it, but I suspect that without loving touch, aging is accelerated. RetroAge changes that. If you give your skin even half as much attention as infants and young children get, you'll have beautiful skin too!

The remedy for touch deprivation lies, quite, literally, in your hands. Make sure to massage, knead, rub, and even scratch your skin while you're in the shower or bath. After drying yourself, begin a rigorous rubdown with natural oils and moisturizers.

Whenever you can swing it, have professional massages. I'll forego a restaurant meal, theatre tickets, or even a gorgeous outfit to afford my weekly massages. Doesn't sound like I'm making any huge sacrifices, but even in hard times, I've found inexpensive, and even free, massage therapists to take care of me. You can too. Check out schools and special offers at spas.

YOUR SKIN IS THIRSTY

The third component of skincare is **Hydration.** Water, that precious fluid that carries youth-giving nutrients into our tissues, is the single most important element in preventing cells from becoming dry and aged. The hydration process is achieved internally by drinking spring or filtered water, herbal and caffeinated tea, freshly squeezed juices along with eating a diet rich in *raw* fruits and vegetables.

Externally, your daily post-shower massage with 100% pure moisturizers helps provide the hydration your skin craves. Yes, every day! People usually fight with me on this one saying they have no time for all this "stuff." They've even been known to tease me by calling me a "pampered princess." Of course, I retort by assuring them that spoiled or not, this "princess" has great skin. Then I urge them to follow my lead and set aside the time to take care of themselves. Give yourself the time to get young! Your body will thank you for it.

Skin is blessed with an astounding capacity to regenerate. Thankfully, there is no time in life that this process stops. Yes, it's true, aging may slow it down, but RetroAge Skin Care revs it up to childlike speed.

RETROAGE SKIN CARE BASICS

Here are some basic techniques of your daily RetroAge Skin Care Regime:

- **Dry and Wet Brush** *your entire body.*
  Speeds up Mother Nature's exfoliation process for younger, smoother skin.
- **Massage** *your muscles from head to toe.*
  Increases circulation and vitalizes skin and muscle tone.
- **Drink** *filtered or spring water, tea and unsweetened juice each day.*
  Maintains supple, dewy skin and keeps it hydrated.
- **Bathe** *in a tub of warm water with aromatherapy oils and sea salts.*
  Totally relaxes your body and relieves stress while cleansing the skin of youth-stealing toxins.

LOTIONS AND POTIONS

Almost any face cream can make you look more youthful... temporarily. What makes skin care products work on a long-term basis is their purity. While costly products may contain extraordinarily beneficial ingredients, using relatively inexpensive products can also give you excellent results. According to the FDA, all crèmes must contain some preservatives. The best companies use Vitamins C and E, which are natural anti-oxidants.

Regardless of the price range, check the labels and make certain that they contain no mineral oils, petroleum products, sodium laurel sulfate, propyl or isopropyl alcohol, parabens, or artificial coloring or scents. These are readily absorbed by the skin and can cause premature aging and potentially serious threats to the immune system.

I use a blend of natural essential oils and organic plant-based moisturizers, formulated by my aromatherapy chemist. My original, custom blend, INCREDIBLE EDIBLE BODY BUTTER, is, of course, my favorite. For cleansing, Dr. Bronner's liquid soap, which is as pure as it gets, is my choice. I love the lavender–scented one, and even use it as shampoo. Then I follow it with a chemical-free conditioner that I buy in my local health food store.

My role of thumb: If it's advertised on TV or is a big seller at the drug store, avoid it like the plague. In fact, I never purchase any shampoo, soap or skin care product at a pharmacy, supermarket or drug store. Nowadays, with all the hype about "Organic", I'm even careful when I shop at a health food store.

Hattietude: If you can't pronounce it... don't use it!

FACES NEED MASSAGE TOO!

The secret to great skin is not simply the ingredients of your cream or even a healthy diet. I've found that TOUCH is the answer. And what kind of touch? I answer that with another of my "weird" recommendations:

No matter what you've been warned, I don't recommend being gentle when you're applying your cream, or when you're washing off your make-up. Get in there and stimulate your face with your fingertips and your palms. Careful of those nails, you don't want to break skin. **Press hard** against the skull and **feel the pressure.**

Just in case you're worrying that this could be bad, and possibly even dangerous, I want to assure you that there's no cause for worry. Deep massage doesn't damage the skin. On the contrary, pressure is beneficial to your face and neck and helps create glowing skin and re-vitalized facial muscles.

You may even go further and join me in pinching the skin. Yes, pinching! This too might also seem strange at first. You're probably thinking, "I can't do that. If I pinch or pull at my skin, it'll stretch and sag." That might be true if you only contacted the surface skin, but when you work deeply, you are stimulating the muscles and connective tissue underneath the skin. This improves circulation and helps your skin regenerate.

I've pressed, pulled and pinched my skin for years, and so have several of my clients and friends. Doing this, along with my *Lift That Face*™ exercise routine, has given us enviably youthful faces.

TOUCH YOUR FACE TO BEAUTY

Has it ever occurred to you that the places our bodies wrinkle the most are the very one's we've been cautioned not to touch? We're constantly told to be careful with our faces, especially the delicate skin around our eyes. How often have we heard that we must never push and pull at our face... or else!

When I hit my forties, my neck started to look crepe-like. I might have been able to ignore this "predictable" sign of aging, but my then teenaged daughter, Rama, always eager to keep me on target, strode up to me, touched my neck and groaned. Her not-so-subtle reminder made me realize I had better do something fast.

I had already determined that cosmetic surgery would never be an option - a decision I hold to this day. But I didn't want to have an old-looking, wrinkly neck either. The skin from my chest down looked terrific, so I wondered why my neck and face were aging faster than the rest of my body. I asked myself if I were doing something below my shoulders that I wasn't doing from the shoulders up. I realized that though I exercised my entire body daily, I was leaving out my face and neck. I decided to experiment by including my face and neck in my daily workout. To my delight, the more I pinched, pressed and even rigorously brushed my face and neck, the less wrinkly they became. Age spots started to fade, and my skin began to glow.

What a nice surprise!

Don't think I was lightly tapping with my fingertips or using feather-light strokes either. I was pinching hard enough for my skin to become pink and pressing deeply enough to reach the muscle tissue below. I even rubbed my eyelids and under my eyes really hard, which is a definite no-no if you believe generations of "experts."

Then I created a series of *LIFT THAT FACE!* exercises for toning and lifting the face. I hope you enjoy doing them. They're easy, and rather cute, if I say so myself!

THE *LIFT THAT FACE!* ™ EXERCISE ROUTINE

Some of these LIFT THAT FACE! exercises look kinda odd, so you might want to start doing them in private. No one will laugh at you there - and they certainly won't be laughing when they see the results. They'll probably even join in.

My theory is that the more you work muscles, the healthier they become. Allow your face to be animated, to smile, grimace, and even frown. Unlike a balloon or a rubber band, facial muscles will not become permanently stretched out.

Here we go!

Hattietude: An animated face is an interesting face!

ABOUT YOUR *LIFT THAT FACE!*™ ROUTINE

1. *Before you start, apply cream all over your face, making sure you lavish it around the eyes, lips and neck.*

2. *Do your Lift That Face! exercises while looking in the mirror to make sure you aren't creating any new wrinkles or distorting your face while you're doing them.*

3. *Start with ten of each exercise and work up to doing fifty of each. Once you've learned to do them properly, you can do them any time, any place, without a mirror. While watching television is a good time.*

4. *Do these exercises daily if you can. If not, start with every other day. Once you see the results, you might decide to exercise your face as routinely as you brush your teeth.*

5. *Don't worry about overdoing it. Unlike motor muscles that carry your body from one place to another, these are not weight–bearers. They thrive with the workout.*

BE CHEEKY

My voice teacher pointed out that opera singers rarely have deep vertical crease lines between the nose and lips. In order to create rich, round tones, they have to form the proper resonating chamber. They do this by pulling their lips forward and working their cheek muscles. This exercise, which I call **PUSH-UPS FOR THE CHEEKS,** will do the same for you:

1. Stand or sit in front of a mirror, keeping your shoulders relaxed.
2. Open your mouth as wide as you can.
3. Firmly press the knuckles of each hand against each cheekbone and pull your lips tightly downward over your teeth as if pretending you have no teeth.
4. Alternate "Ooing" and "Aahing" fifty times. Yes, fifty!
5. Do this exercise when you wash your face in the morning and at bedtime to discourage development of vertical creases between your nose and mouth, and to develop strong cheek muscles.

Does it feel like your face has just gotten a hard workout? You're right. It has!

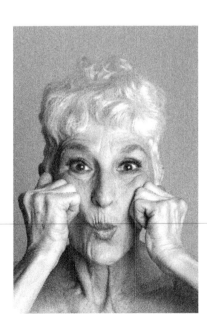 

BLOW-UPS

Another of my favorite cheek vitalizers is called **BLOW-UPS:**

1. Keeping your mouth firmly closed, blow up your cheeks in puffs, like inflating a tire with a pump.

2. Hold for a count of ten; then release. Repeat 10 times.

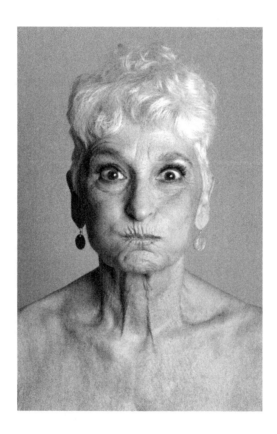

LOVELY LIPS

I want to start this part by saying that I think collagen injections are disgusting and disfiguring. Instead of making the lips look younger, they make them look as if the person was punched in the mouth.

Next is **THE RUBBER BAND -** a fun exercise that corrects or prevents tight lips and a pinched-looking mouth. You'll trade them in for a soft, appealing, youthful look.

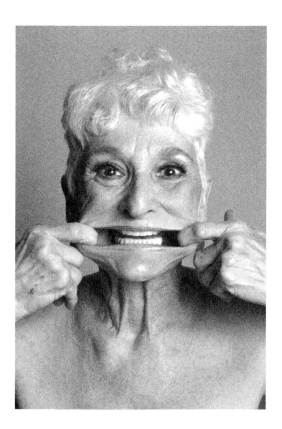

1. Hold your mouth partly open and with your forefingers, pull the corners apart as wide as possible.

2. Then quickly remove the fingers and let the mouth "snap" back to its natural position.

NECKCERCISE™!

I suspect necks age more quickly than faces because we touch them less often. In fact, we generally only wash them when we're taking a bath or shower. How often have you washed your face like it was a mask, stopping at your chin and hairline?

The next time your wash you face, give some attention to your neck as well by firmly pressing the skin under your jaw against the jawbone. This helps prevent a double chin. Next is a pinch/ pull neck vitalizer:

1. Hold your head erect.

2. Grab the skin on your neck with your thumb and forefingers, pinch and pull it.

   Do this daily and you won't ever have to worry about getting a waddle.

EARLOBES

Earlobes? Yes. Earlobes.

One common sign of aging that you may never have considered is droopy earlobes. We rarely give them a second thought, but there they are, waiting to be touched. Give them a mini-workout by massaging them with a skin-softening lotion or oil. This TLC feels nice, too.

ONE MORE THOUGHT

Each day, when you brush your teeth, also brush the insides of your cheeks, your tongue and the roof of your mouth. When the inside is healthy and clean, it shows on the outside.

ABOUT SKIN CARE

- *Do not use petroleum jelly, mineral oil, propyl alcohol, parabens, SLS, or any substances on the body that are not made of the finest, natural, non-chemical cruelty-free ingredients.*

- *Don't be afraid to be rough with your skin. Work deeply enough to energize your muscles, but not so hard as to cause bruising or cause injury.*

- *Keep all your nails groomed, particularly on your feet, so bacteria and fungus don't take up permanent residence.*

- *Pumice and scrape away all your calluses. If you ever develop a huge callous build–up, have it removed by a doctor or skilled manicurist. Don't let yourself grow a crust.*

- *Have professional massages as often as your budget will allow – and take them as deeply as you can comfortably handle. The deeper the strokes, the more effectively they relieve stress and increase circulation.*

- *Never use talcum powder. Instead, use cornstarch, which has no silicon in it. Talc can be damaging to your skin and your lungs.*

PLASTIC SURGERY?   NOT!!!!!

It upsets me to see people having facelifts, tucks and liposuction at younger and younger ages. Personally, I have vowed to never have any cosmetic surgery for any reason, barring a disfiguring accident. This decision is based on my reverence for nature and my spiritual commitment to honor myself as God's child.

The other day I read that both men and women are spending upwards of $15,000 to get their faces lifted because they're afraid they won't be able to get jobs if they don't look young.

This is a sad state of affairs, and one that each of us must battle in our own way. It is my hope that my stand relative to this will encourage others not to yield to what I consider to be a destructive, spiritually flawed decision.

That's how I refer to plastic surgery when I'm seriously confronting the issue. When I'm being less serious, I say, "Face Lifts are like potato chips... you can't have just one!" or "Change the drapes, and the sofa looks old!"

Hattietude: There's beauty at every age. Claim yours, smile, and be grateful!

AND WHAT ABOUT THE SUN?

In this age of holes in the Earth's ozone layer, it's essential that we protect our skin from sun damage. You've often about the dangers of extensive exposure to the sun's rays. However, totally avoiding the sun is not healthy either. You are depriving your body of Vitamin D, which is an essential nutrient for bone growth and repair.

Not often thought about, but at least as important, is the effect of the sun's rays on the center core of bones - the marrow. The bone marrow is the body's white and red blood cell factory. Without direct sunlight it can't produce sufficient cells to keep us healthy, even with Vitamin D supplements. To keep your immune system strong, make sure to take the sun's rays as often as you can, always making sure not to overdo it. Whenever possible, lie in the sun and allow its rays to bathe your skin. Of course, to prevent damage, make it no more than 20 minutes at a time, and never from 11:00 a.m. - 2:00 p.m. I often say to clients, "If you stay out of the sun, it's like expecting a plant to grow in a closet."

Wear a hat with a wide brim especially when you're in direct sunlight. This will not only shade your eyes, but also protect your hair and scalp. Also, optically ground sunglasses with sufficient tint to filter out ultraviolet rays are a valuable addition to your sun protection arsenal. And sunglasses also prevent the squinting that gives us lines around our eyes and furrows on our brow. Who needs those?

EAT PLENTY OF BROCCOLI - IT PREVENTS SUN DAMAGE

Beware of most commercial sun tan lotions. They are filled with chemicals that damage your skin, while purporting to protect it. When you purchase sunscreen make sure it's from a health food store – not one of those over-advertised brands from the drug store that often cause more damage than they prevent.

A word of caution: Avoid wearing perfumes, colognes or scented lotions when you're exposed to the sun. These products, as well as certain medications such as antibiotics, birth control pills and hormone supplements, can cause blotching and uneven coloration.

Several days after sunning, if you haven't gotten burnt, you can help get rid of sun-damaged leathery, dry skin by scrubbing away dead, sun-dried skin while bathing or showering. Yes, you can even scratch it away... I do it all the time!

If you have delicate skin, be careful not to break skin or cause bleeding…rough's good, but not too rough! Then, watch those post-sun dry, dead cells leave your skin and go down the drain. When you're done, apply a non-chemical, natural moisturizer to nourish your freshly exfoliated body. These exfoliating techniques ensure that you'll always have refreshed, glowing, youthful skin.

What a lovely gift to give to yourself.

THE BATHROOM BLITZ

The Blitz assigned to **STEP 3: SKIN CARE** is the Bathroom Blitz. With this one, you'll be throwing away every tube, vial, jar and bottle of skin care, hair care and makeup product that doesn't contribute to your life-long youth.

You may be reluctant to surrender your Vaseline petroleum jelly and baby oil as well as products that contain alcohol, coal tars and synthetic colors. These are the ones you see advertised everywhere. READ LABELS I don't know about you, but when I started reading labels and checking out the ingredients, I was incensed. Paying to be poisoned? No, thanks. As I said before, if it's advertised on TV, it's probably anywhere from useless to dangerous! The only way to get good stuff is to shop at a health food store and restock your arsenal with natural products.

Blitzing your bathroom is a great way to keep your skin care regimen on track. So get out those garbage bags, listen to your favorite music, light a few scented soy candles, and get to work!

CHAPTER NINE
STEP 4...Exercise

I always knew that I wanted the suppleness and endurance of a trained athlete or dancer who works out for hours each day; yet I also knew that I don't have that much self-discipline. I wish I were one of those people who jump out of bed and run off to the gym. I'm not. Luckily, I've found ways to achieve extraordinary results in very little time with activities that I love to do. You can too!

Here we are at the fourth and final **E in E.A.S.E – EXERCISE**

Before industrialization, when physical labor was a part of our lives, we naturally got enough exercise every day. Today, to get adequate exercise, we actually have to plan ways to put movement into our lives. We buy equipment, hire trainers, join gyms and search for the best ways to make sure our bodies are strong and flexible.

The exercises I will be sharing with you have helped me create a younger, more finely toned and flexible body. Along with swimming and dancing, my body is in great shape, easily as fit as many women half my age.

Like most people, I've confronted daunting challenges in the course of my life. There were years in which I was too depressed to be active. I've endured physical and emotional pain that threatened to destroy my life force. But however horrific they were at the time, I have learned to bless all those experiences. Overcoming them has taught me the magnificence of the human spirit and its remarkable capacity for regeneration.

Could I have learned this without pain? I don't know. But I'm thankful that I've been blessed with the courage and drive to keep working towards becoming whole and healthy no matter what life delivers.

There's an expression, "When the student is ready, the teacher shows up!" Thank goodness, healers, teachers, therapists, friends, miracles showed up… and keep showing up. Though I still have pain, you'd never know it from seeing me in action!

That's the beauty of RetroAge!

GETTING TO KNOW YOURSELF

Before we move on, you're going to take yourself on a no-holds-barred tour of your body. With it, you'll stand naked - or at least in your underwear - before a well-lit, full-length mirror and fill out a chart with your observations.

Granted, given the choice, you probably wouldn't do this exercise it at all. But we talked about the value of truth in creating youth. So, I urge you to check yourself out and admit what about yourself you'd like to change. You might even be pleasantly surprised to find aspects of your body that you really like. Good! I hope you keep finding more and more of those.

Over the more than 40 years I've worked with clients and patients, there were probably only three - yes, three – bodies that I thought were what could be called "perfect." One was a model, one an artist and the third a secretary. And you can be sure all three found stuff about themselves that they didn't like. We women are experts at that.

Hattietude: What gets hidden gets ugly!

HOW I VIEW MY BODY

WHAT I HATE	WHAT I DISLIKE	WHAT I LIKE	WHAT I LOVE	I'LL CHANGE

INNERCIZE™ - A NEW WAY TO EXERCISE!

With Innercize you are *sensing* what you are doing while you're exercising. This mental concentration helps your body remember the corrections even when you're not thinking about them. I call this "muscle memory".

SIT UP AND TAKE NOTICE!

Sit sideways in front of the mirror. Don't correct your posture, just sit as you normally do:

Are you slumping?

Is your head tipped forward?

Is your stomach bulging?

Now that you have observed how you ordinarily sit, you're ready to use Innercize to make corrections.

NOW PUT IN THE CORRECTION:

Sit forward on the edge of your seat, without your back contacting the chair.

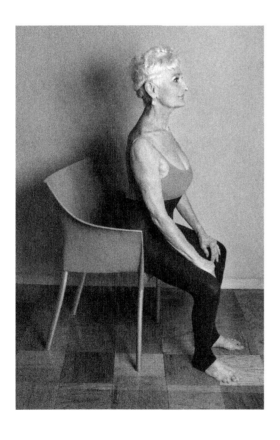

1. Lift your spine as if a string were pulling you up from the top of your head.

2. Keep lifting until you are sitting totally upright.

3. Hold for a count of ten.

4. Slump again and then straighten up. Repeat this slumping and straightening five times.

5. At the end of the fifth time, hold the lifted, upright position for a count of ten.

Sense the feelings in your muscles as you make the correction.

Feels great, doesn't it?

STAND UP FOR YOURSELF!

Stand sideways in front of the mirror. Stand normally and don't suck in your stomach.

Are your knees locked?

Is your back hunched over?

Is your pelvis tipped back and belly protruding?

Are your shoulders slumped or hiked up?

Is your head tilting forward?

Do you look exhausted?

NOW PUT IN THE CORRECTION:

1. Tuck your pelvis forward, tightening your buttocks and bending your knees very slightly.

2. Lift your head and spine so that you feel an upward pull on your torso, as if you're suspended upward.

3. Hold the lifted position for the count of ten.

4. Return to the slumped position, then straighten and slump five times.

5. After the fifth time, hold the suspended position for the count of ten.

Do you feel your spine lifted and your chest more open? Good! Now your breath is deeper, there is less pressure on your lower back, and you feel energized.

INNERCIZE VISUALIZATION... A GREAT HABIT

Each day there are many times when you are just standing still, in an elevator, for example, or waiting in line. Use these downtimes as an opportunity to practice visualization. That way you'll be connecting and correcting just as you did in your mirror exercises.

I have turned waiting time into mini-exercise sessions, as I tighten my stomach and lift my spine while I'm waiting to cash a check or buy some groceries. No one knows why I'm smiling... it's my little fitness secret!

Throughout the day and during your routine activities, whenever you become aware that your body is drooping, slumping or tense, breathe deeply, lift yourself up and continue with your with Innercize Visualization.

Ask yourself:

Is my head jutting forward?

Am I looking down at the ground?

Am I taking small, cautious steps?

Are my arms stiff, as if I'm afraid I might fall?

From this point on, monitor yourself throughout the day. When you become unconscious of your posture or gait, aging takes over. Then it's important for you to quickly counter these tendencies with Innercize.

Practice Innercize in front of a mirror for two weeks to re-program your muscles.

FLEXIBLE FOREVER!

The major difference between children's bodies and adults' is that children move with abandon. They bend and unbend effortlessly, fall and are not seriously injured. However, at about the age of twenty... yes, that early... the muscles start to tighten up and our natural movement starts slowing down. That creates a vicious cycle. Your joints are stiff so you move less. Then you become even less flexible. This in turn inhibits free movement, and around it goes again and again. RetroAge Exercises help break this cycle.

RETROAGE EXERCISE BASICS

- ***Make sure you keep breathing throughout each exercise.***
  Most people hold their breath when they exercise. It's a good idea to sing, hum, count, sigh, and even groan. Making sounds will help you keep breathing.

- ***Don't lock your knees or elbows.***
  When you tighten your joints, it cuts off circulation and puts pressure on the nerves and bones. You may feel stronger for the moment, but you end up weaker in the long run.

- ***Don't arch your lower back.***
  We automatically pull up our lower backs when we strain, and when we're tired our backs arch on their own. This stresses the discs, causing pain, back problems and, as a final jolt, gives you a potbelly!

- ***Keep your pelvis tilted forward.***
  This releases tension in the buttocks and legs and takes the strain off the lower back.

- ***Do your RetroAge Exercises every day.***
  Learn to enjoy the sensations in your muscles and joints as they become more limber and responsive.

FIVE FOR FLEXIBILITY

The following Five RetroAge Exercises work to keep your body limber. They also reduce muscle and joint pain and discourage the onset of arthritis and osteoporosis.

#1 SPINE STRETCHER

Great for: Arms, shoulders, spine, circulation, stomach

Starting Position: Stand straight, legs apart, toes forward and knees slightly bent. Sense the soles of your feet contacting the floor and visualize your head and spine lifted.

Actions:
1. Put your arms behind your back and clasp your fingers together.
2. Straighten your arms, pulling your shoulder blades together. Slowly and smoothly start bending forward, leading with the head.
3. Pull your clasped arms as far as you can upward, toward the ceiling. Hold for ten counts.
4. Slowly return to starting position, keeping the hands clasped firmly behind you throughout.
5. Repeat five times. Concentrate on bending lower each time.

Reminder: Keep pelvis tipped forward and buttocks tight the entire time.

Besides making you more flexible, this brings blood to the head and energizes your entire body.

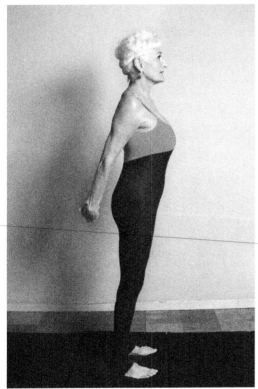

#2 "FROGGY" FLEXER

Great for: Ankles, knees, hips, spine, neck

Starting Position: Stand straight, legs hip-width apart, toes pointed slightly outward, knees loose.

Actions:

1. With head down, slowly bend your knees outward, reaching your hands toward the floor.
2. Continue crouching, bending your knees outward and lowering till you reach the floor.
3. Place palms on floor and lift your head and look forward so you look like a frog ready to leap. Hold this position for a count of five.
4. With your palms still on the floor, start straightening knees slowly and smoothly while lowering your head. Hold in this downward position for a count of five.
5. Slowly lift your torso and head and return to starting position.
6. Repeat five times.

This exercise helps keep your knees and hip sockets supple.

1

2

3

4

#3 TORSO STRETCH

Great for: Hips, spine, torso, arms, neck

Starting Position: Sit on floor with right leg bent at knee in front and left leg to the back, knees bent. Distribute weight evenly on both hips. Hold head high and back straight.

Actions:

1. Reach up with your right arm while placing your left arm across your body, touching the right side of your ribs.
2. Stretch your right arm way up, and bend to the left as far as you can. Imagine your arm tracing a large arc in the air. Pull your head sideways and down.
3. Still holding your right arm upward, return to the starting position, continuing to stretch your arm in a graceful sweeping arc.
4. Reverse leg and arm positions and stretch to the other side.
5. Repeat five times to the right; five to the left.

This is great for maintaining flexibility in the hip sockets and knees. The best part of the side-to-side-rib stretch is that it opens the chest and allows for healthy deep breathing.

By the way… are you smiling? It beats grunting!

#4 TENSION RELIEVER

Great for: Neck, spine, relieving tension and stress

Starting Position: Sit on the floor, cross-legged, hands on knees, elbows out, spine upright with head high.

Actions:

1. Slowly lower head to your left shoulder, leading with the very top of your scalp as if someone were pulling it with a string. Keep shoulders down. Massage right shoulder and neck with left hand to relieve tension.
2. Slowly lower your chin to your chest, then to the right side and finally to the back, emphasizing four points in space – side, back, other side, front. It may help to say, "Right, front, left, back." Then reverse.

All movements should be done slowly and smoothly, without jerking or forcing, especially when moving your head back.

1

2

3

4

#5 HIP RELEASER

Great for: Lower back, abdomen, hips, ankles, legs.

Starting Position: Lie totally relaxed on your back, knees bent and feet flat on the floor.

Actions:

1. Lift right leg, knee bent. Clasp hands below your knee, and pull gently to your chest.
2. Clasp arms behind your thigh. Slowly straighten leg upward. Do not force.
3. When your leg is as straight as you can get it, alternate flexing and pointing your foot five times.
4. Lower leg.
5. Repeat with left leg.

This can be done on a mat or a rug on the floor or in bed as part of your morning stretches.

> **I've given my morning stretches the name "Bedcercizes™"**
> **I like it!**

THE EVERYWHERE ELSE BLITZ!

The Blitz associated with **STEP FOUR: EXERCISE** is the Everywhere Else Blitz. Get out those garbage bags... it's time to go through closets, cabinets, drawers, stashes, and everywhere else you've stored or accumulated stuff.

Be careful not to hold onto items simply because they remind you of days gone by. RetroAge is about being in the NOW!

Once again follow the rule..."If you need it, keep it. Otherwise, toss, toss, toss."

By now I hope it's gotten a lot easier to look at something and delight in getting rid of it, rather than looking longingly at it, wondering if life without it is worth living! Sure, I'm joking, but when I started blitzing my own place, and then the places of my clients, at the onset. it was practically a traumatic event.

That's actually what makes Blitzing so effective. First you resist, then you give in, then you let go, then you laugh!

Kinda like love!

Make sure you have enough jumbo garbage bags and heavy-duty garbage cans within easy reach. You don't want to run out of supplies and have a reason to stop while you're on a roll.

If you're throwing out heavy boxes of books or old clothes and appliances, arrange for them to be carted away the same day you Blitz. Don't let those bags and boxes hang around too long. More throwaways than you can imagine have found their way back onto a closet shelf or into a freshly blitzed basement simply because they were waiting for a pickup. Get 'em out as fast as you can.

Then breathe a sigh of relief.

CHAPTER TEN
Being "UnInsultable!"

When I first began to be vocal about being young forever, I suspected that my style of relating to aging in a new, sexy way was going to get a fair amount of criticism. It did. Personally, criticism doesn't bother me terribly much. However, I wanted to make sure that older individuals who are choosing this radical path don't feel insulted, or get emotionally hurt by any derision or insults hurled at them. My challenge was to find a way to protect us from society's negative judgments.

It's called **Being UnInsultable!**

With it, not only do derisive comments lose their power to hurt, they become amusing, and even better, provide increased motivation and courage to live in a more authentic mode.

As adults, we have learned the skills of Political Correctness. Of necessity, we learn to curtail the expression of our feelings. Unfortunately, as we learn these so-called "adult" manners, we also learn to lie. We refrain from saying what we see, think and feel, lest we hurt someone's feelings, cause embarrassment or initiate confrontations.

Continually holding back from expressing your beliefs and feelings will ultimately make you inflexible, and inflexibility is one of the hallmarks of aging. Personally, I've made the choice to cultivate the openness of a child. I say what I feel, and I feel what I say. I'm also not terribly concerned about the consequences. Of course, I'm mindful to avoid being grossly insensitive or cruel. It's just that being truthful and openly expressed are how I want to live.

Naturally, some resented my unbridled candor. But it was also appreciated and enjoyed by others - after they got over the initial shock! Since I didn't curtail my style of expressing myself to others, I also stopped being so sensitive about what others said about, and to, me. No longer did I feel that I had to walk on eggshells to be accepted.

This was also very liberating for my friends who felt freer to be themselves with me. We stopped being super sensitive and super careful. We were living in truth, and it felt great.

It still does!

TRUTH = YOUTH

To arrive at this level of freedom, I practiced accepting anything about myself that was negative or demeaning…in short, INSULTS. So as not to ever have to be defensive, or get my feelings hurt, I sat down and made a list of possible insults that people could say about me. I thought of it this way. If I've thought of it first, then nothing anyone says can hurt me… it won't be anything I haven't already told myself. I was going to be **UnInsultable!**

This is a fun way to help you to never, ever be hurt no matter what anyone says. You'll be shocked at how much these so-called "insults" can teach you about yourself… and about the person flinging them at you. Allowing truths to see the light of day vaporizes their seriousness and releases the stranglehold they have on you.

Can you imagine how liberating it will be to have others express themselves without fearing that they'll hurt your feelings? Besides, no one says you have to agree with them.

Hattietude: Nothing lightens life like laughter!

MY INSULT SHEET

10 TERRIBLE THINGS THAT CAN BE SAID ABOUT ME I've tried to pick insults that could conceivably hurt my feelings. By the time I was finished, it seemed that no one could outdo my nastiness!	RATING
1. You're a repulsive old hag who thinks she's sexy.	9
2. Your theories are bullshit. You're a complete fraud.	10
3. You're one of the weirdest people on Earth.	5
4. You're a hypocrite and hate old people.	10
5. You're getting Alzheimer's, you stupid idiot.	8
6. You look ridiculous when you dance.	10
7. You don't even see your wrinkles and saggy skin.	6
8. Your children would rather you never visit them.	10
9. You're a cheap bitch making believe you're generous.	10
10. Your dreams will never come true. Give up already!	10

Now fill out your own INSULT SHEET. Write down all the "terrible" things you can come up with that would wound your very soul were someone to say them to you. As you write down your hidden horrors, you can actually learn to enjoy whatever criticism is leveled at you. Don't hold back. Be crude and vulgar if that's what's true. Then rate your insults from 1 to 10, with 1 being a mild sting and 10 being a major "ouch." Go for the "ouches".

10 TERRIBLE THINGS THAT CAN BE SAID ABOUT ME	RATING
1.	
2.	
3.	
4.	
5.	
6.	
7.	
8.	
9.	
10.	

CHAPTER ELEVEN
Age Power

Here I am, in my 70's, vital, beautiful, and spiritually evolved. But despite these attributes, I am faced with what I believe is the most powerful and destructive "ism" that still exists - ageism. Far be it from me to collapse and fall apart under this unjustified prejudice. I realized that we older people have the divine opportunity to inspire the young... I call that AGE POWER!

Everyone starts out young... and of course, we all get old. When I was a teen-ager, and on into my twenties, I feared aging, but felt immune to it. I would look at old people and wonder how they let themselves get that way... as if they made a wrong turn somewhere.

Then, I became an old person myself. I knew that it was an important choice to make. I could either find a way to make aging wonderful, or spend my life suffering, *kvetching* and complaining... no fun at all!

Rather than discouraging me, our society's contempt for older people lit a fire under me. I set out to counter the dreadful belief system that has people disrespect themselves as they get older. It was time to show the world that self-respect and self-love *at every age* is crucial to the survival of our planet.

That's quite a sweeping statement - survival of our planet. Let me explain how I made this connection.

It's easy to love what's exquisite, beautiful and perfect. Our divine task, as individuals and as a society, is to love and honor ourselves and the gift of life even when it *isn't* these things.

Few older people feel fantastic about being old. I guess that's natural. But rather than discouraging us, the very negativity that depresses us can also motivate us.

Remember the "Creative Self-Disgust" I talked about? Hating aging can enable us to become even more resolute about changing the destructive view that society has handed us. Then we can become inspirations for young people, who will one day be old themselves.

What a gift this will be for generations to come!

Hattietude: Our greatest power is to empower the young!

It's not only older people who experience self-hatred. Remember how critical you were of yourself when you were growing up? Even though you weren't worrying about aging, you were constantly discontent about something... your hair, your nose, the shape, size or location of your breasts. You were too tall or too short, too thin or too fat, too busty or too flat chested, too stressed or too laid-back. Ring a bell?

As humans we keep searching for the reasons for our sadness and our fears, and it's so easy to place the blame on aging. I believe that we are suffering from an epidemic of self-hatred with aging being a prime target of this malice. We have the opportunity to turn that cryptic view around.

I often have to remind myself that we are all bound by the same life forces. Like the tides, we rise and fall. In truth, there is little difference between being young and being old. Life is magnificent, and monstrous, at various turns.

We've survived so much, and learned so many valuable lessons along the way. Rather than yearning for the past, our years of growing and learning can be used to enhance all life on Earth. That's where your AGE POWER comes in! Give yourself time for this new way of being to flower.

I often muse about how long it took me to become whole and healthy. Wouldn't it be a shame if I didn't have the stamina to enjoy my hard-earned sanity? Fortunately, RetroAge has given me the means to achieve lifelong youthfulness, and I fully intend to enjoy it well into my eighties... nineties... who knows?

As you open yourself to the possibility of growing in depth, compassion and joy with each passing year, you will meet more and more people on this wondrous path. They will welcome and help you, and you, in turn, will welcome and help others.

We humans have that opportunity.

It can create our glory… or our doom.

The choice is ours.

Hattietude: Youth isn't wasted on the young…
or on anyone else!

CHAPTER TWELVE
Words From My Heart

I thought that I was just trying to look younger and sexier, but my RetroAge journey delivered me an unexpected bonus. I have watched myself transform from an often frightened sometimes foolish, less than courageous older woman into a glowing example of personal integrity and inspiration.

RetroAge has extended my life far beyond the borders of my Being.

Suddenly I found myself resurrecting dreams that I abandoned years before as unattainable or impossible. I even got butterflies in my stomach when I decided to move to a Caribbean island without a job, savings or friends. And who could possibly have predicted that 20 years after winning Roseland's Bathing Suit Beauty Contest that I would be cast as a cougar in a Dolce & Gabbana ad for VOGUE, Harper's Bazaar, Vanity Fair and W in a skin tight gold bathing suit?

And, that's not all.

I have become the embodiment of my most treasured belief – that beauty, love, compassion and contribution to Humanity are attributes that grow through Time.

Out of fear comes courage.

Out of hatred comes love.

Out of dreams come action.

Out of action comes miracles.

YES, it takes courage.

YES, it is hard work.

But most important…

Life is filled with miracles… and you are one of them!

Hattietude: Impossible = I'm possible!

AFTERWORD

After completing all the writing, I called in my fabulous photographer, Zoila Suarez, to take new shots for this updated book.

Whenever we work together, we have a wonderful time, with reggae music and singing and laughter accompanying the clicks of her camera.

This time, as in the past, I felt ready and relaxed, especially since Zoila captures my "look" and the photos are always strikingly beautiful. Unretouched and hardly posed, they look like the me I see in the mirror each day.

But when I reviewed the final shots I was taken aback! Wrinkles on my chest and my arms? Who knew they were lurking there?

My first response was, "I'd better call Zoila back for another shoot. This time we'll concentrate on taking only the most flattering angles with the best lighting and make-up, and toss out any that don't make me look spectacular."

A huge dose of EGO had emerged.

Recognizing my own vanity, I had to admit that I was being as self-hating and critical of my own aging as I've been telling everyone else not to be! What a wonderful revelation!

I stared at the shots and at my naked body, and a huge smile appeared on my face. This is how I look in my seventies... and it's just fine with me! There would be no reshoot.

Some wrinkles? Yes!
Some hanging skin? Yes!
Some lack of tone? Yes!

And what emerged as the most resplendent "Yes" of all?

Yes to understanding and appreciating that life-long renewal awaits us all. All we need do is respect and love ourselves, others, and the gift of life.

We each have within us the capacity for exquisiteness of Being. Therein lies eternal youth and beauty!

WHO IS HATTIE ANYWAY?

In her seventies, a time when most people are slowing down, Hattie is turning the tide by challenging the current paradigm of aging in America. Embodying characteristics generally reserved for women decades younger, she has positioned herself as an example of radiant health, beauty and sexuality for both young and old alike. She proves over and over again that *anyone* can be a victor over time, not its victim.

With her international lecturing career and her ground-breaking book: *The Complete Idiot's Guide to Looking and Feeling Younger*, Hattie has earned a reputation as a sought-after expert on maintaining lifelong youth. She holds a registered trademark, *RetroAge* that embodies her radical approach to reversing aging.

At 52, wearing a super-revealing swimsuit, she won first prize in New York's Roseland Over-50 Bathing Suit Beauty Contest. Appearing in the same suit the next morning, an astonished Regis announced, "There she goes. An inspiration to all of America!" Her appearances on *Fox Magazine* and *NY 1* have inspired millions of TV viewers and she was the only senior ever to appear topless on the *Howard Stern Show*. In December 2008, at 72, she appeared as the consummate cougar in VOGUE, HARPER'S BAZAAR, W and VANITY FAIR in a gold bathing suit, holding hands with a 20 something hunk!

Her background in modern dance with Martha Graham, psychoanalytic psychotherapy studies at the National Psychoanalytic Institute for Psychoanalysis (NPAP), along with her heritage as a healer, uniquely qualify Hattie to confront aging from a combined physical, psychological, and spiritual perspective.

Now in her seventh decade, Hattie's unprecedented youthfulness and vibrant beauty - without cosmetic surgery or shots - insure Hattie's role as an authentic role model for women everywhere. Her life-affirming *"Hattietudes"* impart a radically positive view of aging that inspires future generations to honor themselves at every stage of life.

HATTIE IN THE MEDIA

Sunday, April 11, 2004

The New York Times

The City

WHO'S WHO

ダブリュー・ジャパン
W JAPAN

The perfect gift for the Ladies

THE SETTING: As you sit nursing a cranberry spritzer at the dimly lit Coda lounge on a balmy Tuesday night, you don't notice it at first, but the music being piped into the bar is all about heartache: Patsy Cline's "I Fall to Pieces," Cyndi Lauper's cover of "Until You Come Back to Me," John Lennon's "I'm Losing You."

This is not surprising, because this particular evening the main attraction at Coda, at Madison Avenue and 34th Street, is the Break Up Club. Billed as "entertainment therapy," the event is equal parts cabaret and consolation, and this evening a score of suddenly single New Yorkers, at least half of them in their 40's, have come to talk about their heartbreak into a mike and then belt it out on stage karaoke-style.

THE BUZZ: "Consider this your emotional embassy," said Buddy Winston, the evening's architect and M.C., as

Michael Nagle for The New York Times

Dancing their blues away at the Break Up Club.

年を重ねることは素晴らしい
それを教えるのが私の人生の意義

metro

SPECIAL WEEKEND SECTION   NEW YORK SEPTEMBER 23-2

PEOPLE

Condé Nast TRAVELER · August

celaviclei.com

Condé Nast

PULLOUT GUIDE TO
LAS VEGAS

2005

WIN! A TRIP FOR TWO

Hattie, 69,
"Miss Roseland"

ThursdayStyles

The New York Times

N   G1

THURSDAY, NOVEMBER 15, 2007

WHAT PEOPLE ARE SAYING

"Once in a while you meet someone who is not afraid to take chances, who keeps on enlarging her cycle of life and goes on to other things. Hattie... an inspiration to all of America. God bless you. You look fabulous!"

Regis Philbin, "Mr. Television"

"Hattie, I wish I can look like you when I'm your age."

Paula Zahn, award-winning newscaster

"Your talent and energy were absolutely infectious! You are a pleasure to work with."

Geraldine Newman, President, NEWTHYNK

"You are an outstanding member of the Holistic Movement. We are delighted to have you with us each year."

Mark Becker, Founder, New Life Expo

"Hattie offers a breakthrough to the affirmation of life, plus the vitality to share it with all humankind."

John P. Kildahl, Ph.D., Clinical Psychologist

"You have the body of a 20 year-old!"

Albert Knapp, M.D., 50 Top Doctors in New York

"... riveting, authentic and certainly courageous."

Carole Hyatt, CEO, The Carole Hyatt Leadership Group

"Hattie delivers!"

John Russell, Director of Director of Development & Strategy, QVC

"Your energy and enthusiasm are an inspiration to all of us."

Penny Ekkert, Feature Editor, Playboy Magazine

"Your story is truly incredible. You're one of a kind!"

Denise Sylvestro, Senior Editor, Berkley Press

HATTIE A SWIMSUIT BEAUTY QUEEN
THEN... AND NOW.

RoseLand

Same suit...Retroaged Body!

Golden boldie

At 52, Winning Miss Roseland
Bathing Suit Beauty Contest

As Hattie says, "Never forget the YOU in youth!"

ARE YOU SERIOUS?

ABOUT LOOKING, FEELING & *BEING* YOUNGER BY REVERSING THE NEGATIVE EFFECTS OF AGING!

I want one beautiful thing for you: the benefits of **life-long youth**!

Benefits like:

- More energy and vitality

- Radiant, sensual, toned skin

- Increased libido

- Greater flexibility

- A trimmer body

- Better, more robust, health

- Fewer facial wrinkles

- And, quite possibly, a longer, more vibrant life

I invite you to join me on a life-transforming journey to turn aging into an adventure, an opportunity and a gift.

Please place your name on my mailing list so that I can keep you informed about cutting-edge Anti-Aging ideas, technologies and products. Additionally, I will be announcing special cruises, and international Rejuvenation Vacations.

www.hattieretroage.com

SOURCES AND FORCES

People often ask me what products I take in my quest for youth. Here is an abbreviated list of the companies whose products I literally couldn't live without.

WHOLE WORLD BOTANICALS: For indigenous, organically raised herbs from Peru

www.wholeworldbotanicals.com - 877.885.5517

DREAMOUS CORPORATION: Source of homeopathic Human Growth Hormone

www.dreamous.com

KLABIN MARKETING: Longevity Science Ant-Aging and immune system enhancing supplements

800.933.9440

SOUTHALL RESEARCH INSTITUTE: Hyssop herb in many forms, including lozenges.

800.228.4425

WILDERNESS FAMILY NATURALS: Superb coconut products plus numerous other splendid offerings

www.wildernessfamilynaturals.com - 800.945.3801

ARDATH AROMAS: Top quality skin care aromatherapy products

www.ardatharomas.com

MEDICINE FLOWER: Organic, steam distilled aromatherapy oils and variety of pure body products

www.medicineflower.com

AEROBIC LIFE: Oxygen products and Vegan Supplements

www.pure-vegan.net - 800.798.0707 ext 1

GERIVITOL: Romanian Procaine formula for longevity

www.millennium.com

BIOTEC FOOD CORP: Source of anti-oxidants and sea plasma supplements

800.788.1084

PHYSIOLOGICS: Selection of vegetarian vitamins and mineral supplements in glass bottles
www.physiologics.com - 800.765.6675

HIGHER BALANCE INSTITUTE: Eric Pepin's chakra-based spiritually enlightened CDs

www.higherbalance.com

DR. DANA COHEN: holistic integrative medical practice

www.drdanacohen.com

DR. KEITH BERKOWITZ: weight loss and chelation therapy

212.459.1700

DR. FRANCIS CLIFTON: holistic psychotherapy and visualization

212.354.4373

SILVERLINING INTERIORS: Impeccable interior construction, offering green building and toxin-free materials
www.silverlininginteriors.com - 212.496.7800

BOOKS:

Ageless Body, Timeless Mind………………………………………….. Deepak Chopra

Diet for a New America………………………………………………….John Robbins

In Defense of Food………………………………………………….. Michael Pollan

Natural Cures "They" Don't Want You to Know About…………………..... Kevin Trudeau

Diagnostic Face Reading and the Holistic You……………………………Roger Bezanis

Beauty To Die For………………………………………………………….Judi Vance

Order Hattie's exciting and inspiring memoir:

Sex And The Single Senior
A Cougar's Search For Love

www.hattieretroage.com

Printed in Great Britain
by Amazon

79436695R00075